From The Files Of A Sex Therapist

T0097416

From
The Files
Of A Sex
Therapist

by Carole Altman, Ph.D.

Lifetime Books, Inc.

Copyright © 1998 by Carole Altman.
All rights reserved. Published by Lifetime Books, Inc., 2131 Hollywood Boulevard,
Hollywood, FL 33020. Phone: 1-800-771-3355.
http:www//lifetimebooks.com; e-mail: lifetime@shadow.net

Reproduction, translation, or use in any form by any means of any part of this work beyond that
permitted by Section 107 or 108 of the 1976 United States Copyright Act without the permission of the copyright owner is unlawful. Requests for permission or further information should
be addressed to the Permissions Department, Lifetime Books, Inc., 2131 Hollywood Boulevard,
Hollywood, FL 33020.

This publication is designed to provide accurate and authoritative information in regard to the
subject matter covered. It is sold with the understanding that the publisher is not engaged in
rendering legal, accounting, or other professional service. If legal advice or other assistance is
required, the services of a competent professional person should be sought. *From A Declaration
of Principles jointly adopted by a Committee of the American Bar Association and a Committee
of Publishers.*

Library of Congress Cataloging-in-Publication Data
Altman, Carole.
  From the files of a sex therapist / by Carole Altman.
    p. cm.
  ISBN 0-8119-0874-7
    1. Sex therapy--Popular works. 2. Psychosexual disorders--Popular works. I. Title.
  RC557.A46 1998
  616.85 ' 8306--dc21   98-6770
                                                                             CIP
Interior Design by Vicki Heil
Cover Photo by Telegraph Color Library/FPG International
10 9 8 7 6 5 4 3 2 1

Printed in Canada

Table of Contents

Sex therapists must be desensitized. Sex therapists must learn about: The Dysfunctions, The Leather Crowd, Homosexuality, Sexual Satisfaction for Paraplegics, Transvestites and Transsexuals, Cunnilingus and Fellation, The Sex "Muscles," Love, Non-Judgementalism and Acceptance

You will look into the minds and hearts of my clients, as well as my own, to see a clear picture of what therapy is and why it works.

Maryann & Burt:
Burt's need to wear make-up and silk undergarments almost ruined their marriage.

Julia & Tim:
Julia needed to camouflage her wild and aggressive sexuality by pretending to be a "lion." She needed to trust Tim so that she could share this with him; he needed to love her enough to enjoy the "lion" within her.

Janet & Greg:
Janet's vaginismus was a psychological reaction to Gregg's plan to move to England. Their inability to have sexual intercourse challenged Gregg's love and almost ended their marriage.

Bob & Lillian:
The reprehensible tortures which Lillian suffered as a child had created a need in her to be hurt. Lillian's disclosure of her abuse, and Bob's reactions helped them to begin the road to recovery.

Penny & Charles
Charles' impotence was a shock. The atmosphere of intense anger and blame between them was corroding their marriage. The cause of his impotence was even more of a surprise.

Renee & Paul:
Renee's high sex drive collided head-on with Paul's. As her demands intensified, his interest diminished. Mutual satisfaction was the goal as they found their solution.

Bill & Sara:
Sara was increasingly frustrated with Bill's lack of sexual knowledge and experience. Bill needed not only to learn how to satisfy Sara's needs, but more importantly, how to overcome the childhood taboos so deeply ingrained in them.

Rob & Joan:
At first Joan accepted Rob's fetish which required that stockings be a part of their lovemaking. But she began to worry that Rob's fetish was sick.

Stan & Cynthia:
"Is it alright if Cynthia expels an egg from her vagina while I cluck like a chicken? It excites us and we like it. What do you think?"

Helen & Dick:
Is playing "mommy and daddy" a dangerous sexual game?

Sandy & Randall:
"Is playing 'pick-up' dangerous? We really enjoy sex if we pretend we don't know each other, and then go home as though it's a one night stand. Is this OK?"

Beverly:
"Will using my vibrator inhibit any pleasure I have with a man?"

Harold:
"It upsets me because my wife wants to use a vibrator. What's wrong with me?"

Judy & Ivan:
Judy refused to experience anal sex and Ivan said he "needed" anal sex. The solution to their dilemma was inevitable.

Ingrid:
I was mandated to inform Child Protective Services when Ingrid informed me what she was doing with Darren, her four-year-old son.

CHAPTER III: THE FAILURES & THE TRAGEDIES

Some of the brave and wonderful people who came to see me were not able to succeed. I was part of their failure. They were, in the end, victims of themselves. Read about these tragedies with the realization that if you are willing to work hard, hold on hard, and take control of your life — success will be yours. It's your choice.

Krisy:
Sexually abused, feeling worthless, Krisy ruined her life choosing men she "deserved," who were as worthless and filthy as she herself felt.

Sharon:
A strikingly beautiful woman unable to accept her own value, Sharon ended her life feeling like the junkyard her father owned.

Debbie:
Bright, beautiful, successful, but unable to separate herself from the Master who made her his slave. Despite torture and neglect, Debbie felt Rock was the only man who could satisfy her, and that she could not live without him. The truth was, she couldn't live with him either.

Ben:
An obsessiveness with cleanliness kept Ben from any close relationships. It's difficult to love a man who keeps washing your body while having sex.

CHAPTER IV: ATTITUDES & BEHAVIORS........... III

We face each day not with a tabula rosa, but with a plethora of beliefs and habits which we are often unaware of. We don't realize how these affect our behavior, and how they often inhibit us or control us. The achievements of these clients were possible because they each faced their "childhood witches" like David against Goliath. They took control of the childhood demons from their past, and became the adult they wanted to be. The child need not be the father of the man — if the father is not nurturing, loving, and healthy.

Ani & Elliot:
Ani's early training inhibited any sexually aggressive behavior. Elliot's taboos prevented him from responding to Ani's needs.

Eva & Tom:
Eva rejected Tom's attempts for any sexual behavior other than the "missionary" position. She actually neglected her appearance, and became dowdy and unattractive, thinking it would turn him off so that she didn't have to keep rejecting him. Eva told Tom of her mother's frequent admonition; "Remember Eva, you don't want to look like you want something you don't want."

Ellie & Jason

Jason left home when he was just 12 years old. He'd been viciously abused, and watched his parents abuse each other, as well as his siblings. He loved Ellie deeply, and was completely unaware of how the vicious and tenacious hand of his childhood was controlling his present.

CHAPTER V: CONCLUSION

Is sex the big bang, the fireworks and lightning? Sometimes. Is sex ordinary and simple and loving and warm? Sometimes. Is sex essential to your relationship? Sometimes. You will read the truth about sexuality and relationships, and learn all you ever wanted to know about your point of view through the eyes of others. You will learn *your* truths, *your* needs, *your* desires. You will learn how to *Make Life Happen!* And, you will make it happen the way you want it to.

Preface

Imagine being a "fly on the wall" in the office of a sex therapist. *From The Files Of A Sex Therapist* allows you to see the deep secrets, the hidden passions, even the unmentionables by taking you on a trip of fantasy, education, and training, through open bedroom doors, into the sex lives of dozens of people. You will observe their successes and learn how to achieve the same for yourselves.

From The Files Of A Sex Therapist is a how-to book. As you read about the men and women in these pages, you will identify with some, empathize with others and be more understanding of the rest of the world. Hopefully, you will learn from all of the people on the following pages.

The identity of the men and women discussed on these pages has been changed so that they will not be recognized. In addition, to protect my clients, I have worked with my files from 1977 through 1984. None of the records discussed are less than fourteen years old. Ninety-five percent of the people discussed were in my office in 1977 and 1978. As you'll discover in the *TRAGEDIES AND FAILURES*, some of my clients have died. I have taken great care in these pages to protect those who are alive. Because I have lectured for many years, it is my practice to ask permission to share the stories of my clients during these lectures. Therefore, permission was granted by my clients to share their stories. Their adventures towards a more fulfilling and passionate life are a source of pride for them, which they share willingly in order for their stories to help others.

From the Files of a Sex Therapist will not only satisfy your voyeuristic pleasures, it will enable you to communicate better, to change, to seek more rewards in life, to make educated choices and to reach for the gold in everything you do. You will learn how to get what you want, and how to enjoy pleasure when you achieve it. Although it may be a book about THEM, it is for YOU!

*Dedicated to the brave and wonderful people
who trusted me to help them.
My children who supported me and accepted my career
so graciously, even when they were embarrassed.
Imagine if your mother was a sex therapist!
My sister, Betty, who is a great source of
encouragement. My sidekick through it all.
And to Rick, my love, who guided me to writing
and most especially to loving.*

CHAPTER ONE

The Sex School

WHEN I REGISTERED, I was told that the course was called "The Fuck-o-rama." It was a necessary course, so that I could become aware of every level, every type of sexual experience. As a sex therapist, I could not be shocked, surprised, judgmental, or frightened. The purpose of "The Fuck-o-rama" was to "desensitize" students to every form of sexuality. I was told students would be shown, by 80 different films, on 20 different projectors, experiences which patients might tell us about.

Imagine the entire wall is covered with illusions, pictures of various sexual experiences, scenes depicting pain, pleasure, agony, and ecstasy. The other students and I sit on wide steps in a semi-circle in front of a white wall.

Twenty projectors behind us illuminate the world of sex, in varying sounds and sights. We lie against huge comfortable pillows, and we watch the films as part of our "study" program.

A nude man and woman are dancing to Paul Anka's *Having My Baby*. They hold an infant between them. The man bends to nibble at the woman's breast. She holds his hardened penis, as they rock the baby. The scene is loving and lovely, a look of ecstasy shines on their faces.

My eyes move to the right, to another screen on the wall in front of us. A young man is on his knees in the center of a small bed. He is masturbating, his body arched backwards, his head almost touching the heels of his feet. Although this film is silent, the intensity of the boy shouts out at me. He seems to be in pain rather than pleasure. I look away.

I look at the top of the wall and see a young woman with long dark hair and a beautiful face. She is licking the penis of a dog. The penis becomes erect. She takes the dog between her legs inserting the penis into her vagina. The dog begins thrusting into the woman, her legs wide open, high in the air. I look away to another scene; I am uncomfortable, this is not what I call entertainment, or educational. Although I am supposed to be non-judgmental, I do draw the line, and I draw it right here. I look away at another scene. Two men are locked together, mouth to penis, penis to mouth. Their groans are muffled but audible. Behind them, at least six men are in a variety of positions, anally penetrating, masturbating and fellating each other.

A handsome middle aged man is applying lipstick. He puts a dab of mascara on his eyelashes, and brushes his cheeks lightly with a rouge brush. He then puts on a bra and panties. They are silky looking and quite scanty. A woman enters the room and begins to fondle him, kissing and holding him closely. They move to the bed, licking each other's ears, lips and eyes. They seem to be loving and close. Turning to the camera she says, "We've been married for fourteen years. I love that he dresses up for me." As I sit huddled between Joe and his wife Sally, I can't imagine how all of these strange and unusual films could be of any help to any of us.

A nude woman in a wheelchair is rolling a vibrator around her nipples, her belly, and between her legs. She has trouble adjusting the vibrator to a favored spot, barely able to separate her legs enough to fit the vibrator against her clitoris. She succeeds, leans her head back so that only her throat is visible. This film stays with me, invading old stereotypes about handicapped people, their limitations, their abilities, their vital sexuality. I vow I will never discount the sexuality of anyone regardless of their situation and age, be they handicapped, single, gay, blind, whatever. The beauty of this woman's pleasure reinforces my conviction to encourage and support all human beings in their quest for passionate and exciting sex.

A young couple frolicking on the grass spread a blanket and open a picnic basket, as they undress and dance nude in the sun. They begin to make love slowly, intensely, never taking their eyes off each other. She straddles him while

3

holding his face in her hands. Barely moving, contracting her vagina slowly, her buttock muscles revealing her internal movements, she sits atop him, kissing and licking his face. I think this beautiful scene is how it should be when two people make love and immediately correct myself; there are no "shoulds." We all have our own way, and are all loving sexual beings. I make a promise to myself to remember that.

On another screen, a man is on his knees. He is blindfolded, with handcuffs tying his wrists and his arms behind his back. A woman dressed in black leather, six-inch heels, panties and a bra, which exposes her huge breasts, places a rope around his neck and pulls his head forward, until his face falls into a dish. He begins lapping at the contents of the dish. She cracks a small whip with strands of leather at the end, first in the air and then across his back. Welts rising on his naked skin become red and more swollen as he continues lapping at the food. I feel uncomfortable again and wonder if I will ever be able to work with someone who is sexually involved in sadomasochism, bondage or control, as my eyes roam to something more "normal," more palatable.

Although I am aware that exposure to the sexually unfamiliar, unusual or even repulsive is essential, I know that, even though these practices may not be for me, I still have to learn to accept sexual choices of others, not as I think they should be, but as they are.

The next scene my wandering eyes settle on is of a young woman shouting obscenities. Her face contorts into ugly grimaces, her neck swelling with an inner rage as she screams over and over again, "FUCK! FUCK! FUCK!" This continues ceaselessly, as the one word screeches her rage of betrayal and of agony. It is difficult to watch, difficult to hear. The repeated word "fuck" is the most audible of all of the sounds emitting from the wall. At that moment , the word "fuck" takes on the meaning of rage to me; it defines hopelessness and powerlessness, and the cruel feelings of the rage of impotence and helplessness.

The wall is covered with at least twenty images and sounds, a wall of human sexuality in every form however delicious and lovely, however demeaning and tragic. The images go on. As they seem to become more vile and demeaning, I feel more uncomfortable.

Soon another new image emerges. It is imposing, covering a large portion of the center screen. There are many nude men milling around. They turn to a wall in which several holes have been drilled. The holes are lined with a fabric. A disembodied penis is put through one of the holes. One of the men turns to the penis and strokes and licks it. The person to whom the penis belongs is on the other side of the wall and cannot be seen. Another disconnected penis comes through another one of the holes. A tall, thin rather unattractive man begins to stroke the flaccid penis. As it becomes erect, he turns his back and inserts the penis into his anus. As he moves back and forth, his body hitting the wall as he rides the penis, the wall suddenly seems to come alive with penises.

There are at least ten anonymous penises coming through various holes in the wall, which men are stroking and licking, or actually being anally penetrated by. Because the camera allows me to see both sides of the wall, I can see the men on the other side plastered tightly against the wall, their arms above their heads, their thighs pressed against the velvet

5

covered wood. They move their penises into the mouths, anuses or hands on the other side. When satisfied, they move, allowing another to use the hole in the same way.

The words "THE TOILET" abruptly announce the nightclub in New York where the next scene is being filmed. A man is shown as he lies down in a bathtub, which seems to be the signal for other men to urinate on him. He lies there while a seemingly endless number of men cover him with their waste. The picture soon blacks out and is replaced by another. I am unaware that not three months after seeing this, I will attend the first conference on AIDS, and learn that it is in these meeting spots for anonymous homosexual sex, that the scourge of AIDS is being spread, and that upon hearing this, the Gay community would be in an uproar, arguing that AIDS is not a Gay disease. They would fight the closing of these places. Finally though, as hundreds would become ill, these places would close not only by order of the Boards of Health, but from lack of customers. The community would have learned quickly, but not quickly enough. AIDS would kill 500,000 men, women, and children.

To their credit, the scourge of AIDS would not spread within the gay community. They would be the most careful of all groups of people, keeping their own lives and sexual safety under very tight control. It would be among the heterosexuals that AIDS would continue to be a very serious problem. They would feel invulnerable, unmindful of the need to have safe sex and to avoid this fatal disease.

I turn to another corner of the wall, another film. A woman with a towel tied to a bedpost holds the towel with two hands behind her, placing it between her legs. As she mounts the towel and begins to move back and forth, riding the towel at a furiously impatient pace, I think about how I will discuss masturbation with my clients. I want to teach them to love their body, softly, gently, and with appreciation and passion. To the woman on the screen, I want to say, "Slow down, touch your breasts, fantasize, and love yourself as you pleasure yourself."

A voice shouting every obscenity imaginable cuts into my thoughts as it permeates the air. It is a faceless voice, barely male or female. It is shrill, ugly and filled with venom, as it screeches over and over again, "CUNT! SHIT! FUCK! ASSHOLE! DIRTBAG!" I turn to the far right side of the wall, hoping for relief. I am drained, unable to sit any longer to see or hear any more of this. I know this is teaching me, but I'm still uncomfortable. Gratefully, I focus on two children racing in and out of the spray of a lawn sprinkler. Their nude bodies glisten in the sun, their laughter warming the room and clearing the poisons of some of the other vivid pictures still encrypted in my brain.

Relaxed, I turn from the screen with the children. A man has his face on the inner thigh of a woman's legs. Her vagina is spread open by his fingers. He keeps his face as far to the side of her vagina as he can. He is demonstrating how to perform cunnilingus. He licks at the outer labia of her vaginal lips, then opening them, he licks the inner labia. He makes circles with his tongue around the vaginal opening, then around the clitoris. He pulls the clitoral hood away, exposing the clitoris and begins licking it with the very tip of his tongue, so the viewer can see as much as possible. The person whose vagina is being filmed begins to moan with glorious pleasure and the man seems to forget this is a "teaching" film. He moves between her legs as she wraps his head with her knees. Her hands, visible for the first time, clutch at his hair, her knees press against his ears. I feel myself stirred for the first time and wrench my eyes away, since I'm in a classroom with 30 other students. I notice the others, all quiet, very still, some holding hands, others hugging, and even others, like me, who sit separated and upright against the cushions while mesmerized by the films, the intensity of the experience.

On even another screen, a woman beneath a donkey with a huge erection is actually trying to insert this appendage into herself. I turn to another picture, remembering that Catherine the Great, a Russian empress, was actually killed when a horse fell on her. She, too, enjoyed the pleasures of the horse's huge penis.

Another woman is sitting on a man's penis, her back to his face. As she turns to face him, she lies flat on top of him, her movements never varying, only her positions. I hope they will kiss at one point during all of these gyrations; they don't. Again, I feel myself imposing my prejudices on others. I tell myself I must stop, and begin again with a tabula rosa, where there are no judgements, no thoughts, no discriminations.

An elderly couple about 75 or 80 years old, walking in the park in another scene turn off the path they are following. He takes a blanket from his shopping bag and spreads it on the grass, and then joins the woman who is undressing. They undress slowly, very sensually. Their bodies are wrinkled, but shapely; the scene is very loving. As they lay down, they move towards each other with rhythm and warmth, kissing for a long time while holding each other as though swaying to music. They lie on the blanket, and as they move, his erect penis becomes quite obvious. She welcomes the sight with a giggle and a small kiss to the tip of it before he plays with her vagina for a minute and then finally inserts himself into her. The entire film is only minutes long. It is lovely and loving, and certainly encouraging. Again, old stereotypes leave me.

I remember thinking my parents didn't have sex anymore because they were too old. I now know that not only do my parents "do it," they keep "doing it" as long as possible, into their 80's and 90's.

I decide to leave the room, making my way between the others, trying to avoid stepping on pillows or classmates. I move down the stadium-like, very wide steps, strewn with huge comfortable pillows serving as classroom chairs. I move out of the room, and find one of the teachers in her office. She is upset that I have left "The Fuck-o-rama." She explains how important "The Fuck-o-rama" is, since it is designed to expose future sexologists to every sort of sexual experience possible, and to teach me to be professional, non-judgmental, and certainly not shocked. She wants me to return for another hour so that I can see "everything." I explain that I have seen enough and assure her that I will never behave in any manner other than a professional one.

My leaving "The Fuck-o-rama" was the beginning of my distancing myself from the sex school, and some of their ideas. I didn't realize then that this experience would indeed help me to maintain myself as a professional sexologist many, many times. I would indeed hear many unusual and even offensive confessions in the years to come, and realize the worth of the "Fuckorama" frequently. However, three hours of experiencing it was too much to ask.

The SEX SCHOOL was certainly avant guard and extremely helpful in many ways. I doubt if I would ever have understood a patient who is involved in bondage as well as I do, had I not met some of the people who came to the class, such as Tom and Sadie. They both loved the fear and control of being tied, tying, threatening, and making love during and after their "control" sessions. Having lunch with them, listening to their ideas about sex and what they do, brought me to the realization that we are all perfect in our own way, and that my way is not better than theirs, it is just different. Tom and Sadie are passionate, bright, sweet young adults who are like you and me – but with different "turn-ons." They earned my respect as well as my curiosity, and dissipated all of my views and critical outlooks about bondage.

However, meeting Steve and Lorie was a different story. Their "master-slave" relationship was one which I viewed as "unhealthy," and one which I, as a therapist, would not encourage. Steve and Lorie were great people, but their sexual choices were pain and torture. Steve actually cut Lorie as she begged for more cuts, deeper and longer. She felt if she showed she could bear the pain for Steve, she would be proving her love for him and her own strength.

You can call me judgmental, that's OK, because, when it comes to this type of sexuality, I am judgmental. I still feel that if you are not hurting yourself or anyone else, either emotionally or physically, then your choices are alright. When destructiveness and pain are involved, though, I say NO, and will try to change your ideas and your behavior.

In class I met quadriplegics who had lost all sensation in their genitals and learned that with proper stimulation to other "live" areas of the body, they could be orgasmic, feeling the same pleasures which a genital orgasm produces. Working with handicapped men and women, helping them to resume their sexual lives was very rewarding. In fact, I now use the same techniques with all of my clients. They help us to expand our sensuality and sexuality by enhancing our sensations in every part of our bodies. We are born polymorphous perverse, feeling pleasure on every inch of skin and follicle of hair. Somehow we begin to concentrate on small areas, the genitals and the nipples. You can actually experience pleasure from a facial massage, touching nothing other than your partner's face, and from sucking on toes and fingers, or stroking the tender skin behind the knees or inside your elbows. You can feel the exquisite delight of touching the neck and throat, the inner thigh and the palm. Learning the techniques of re-establishing sexual responses helped me realize we can all expand our sensuality.

I also met transvestites and transsexuals. I can appreciate what it means to a person to go through the agony of surgery involved if you NEED to change sex. And, I stress — it is a NEED. No one does this by choice. They are truly trapped in the body of someone who is not their sex, but of the opposite sex. The female has a double mastectomy. Her clitoris is then enlarged with the hormone testosterone and her vagina is closed. The skin lining the vagina is taken outside the body

ll

and formed into two testicles. This skin is very sensitive and experiences the pleasure of touch as does the inside of a vagina. The clitoris can grow to about two inches and is sensitive and sexual.

The male has his penis and testicles removed, and the skin is inserted into the cavity just behind the testicles. Although this forms the lining of a "vagina" and can be penetrated as with any vagina, it is not as deep. The skin of the testicles remains as sensitive inside the "vagina" as it did on the testicles. The male also takes progesterone to decrease hair growth, change his voice and increase breast size.

The transvestite, on the other hand, is not as tortured inside the body of the wrong sex. In fact, some transvestites are truly masculine or feminine; they just enjoy dressing in opposite fashion.

I met Jerry, a 6'4" football player, who is "Tarzan" masculine. He and his wife had been happily married for nine years when they came to the sex school to teach us about transvestites. Jerry was wearing an orange chiffon skirt and long matching blouse, earrings, and beautifully applied makeup. He explained that he liked looking this way sometimes and that he also liked to wear a padded bra, silk nightgown and perfume while he and his wife made love. Although he enjoyed what he called "the softness of being feminine," he never wanted sex with a man, or had any interest in them in any intimate way. Jerry loved his wife and appreciated that she accepted his transvestism, his own style of pleasure. Meeting Jerry helped me to understand my future clients.

Along with his wife, Jerry visited our school with Tina, a 6'2" dominatrix. She was dressed in stereotypic fashion with leather shorts, high leather boots, and a short cropped leather shirt. Her blonde hair was pulled back with a leather band and she actually carried a "cat-o-nine-tails," which she slapped against her thigh high boots from time to time. Tina tried to convince us that domination was very important to many people. She said it helps to ameliorate any guilt you may have, because you allow yourself to be punished for anything you do.

Interestingly, research shows the majority of professionals who visit S&M parlors, are lawyers. Can we extrapolate from this information that lawyers are the most guilty, needing to be punished in this way? Who knows?

After their lectures, Jerry, Tina and several of the students and teachers went for lunch at a local restaurant. Imagine the scene: Jerry, a 6'4" man in orange chiffon; Tina, a 6'2" blonde in black leather carrying a whip; and six or seven others all waiting to be seated. Of course, people were staring at us. Incredulously, Tina asked, "Why is everyone looking at us?" I couldn't help my response as I laughingly asked, "Are you kidding, have you looked in the mirror today?" She laughed, too, as Jerry said, "It's really me they're staring at, dominatrixes are a dime a dozen in this town."

The sex school was exceptionally helpful in the "hands-on" experience that it offered. It was so much more real to meet hookers, fetishists, homosexuals and bi-sexuals, the S&M and bondage crowd, the group sex addicts, and the others, than to read about them in cold clinical, analytical books. The experience was invaluable and has helped me throughout the years to be more compassionate, understanding, and accepting of my clients. My experiences at the sex school were rewarding and upsetting, exciting, and depressing. Although much of what occurred, and what I learned was not acceptable to me, it has been an invaluable help.

Although I went on to receive my Ph.D. at a more traditional school, via more traditional avenues, I will always treasure some of my experiences there. One "man" who came to one of the classes had a double mastectomy, but did not change "his" genitals from a vagina to a penis. Now living as a man, Terry joked that "he" was the perfect test for bi-sexuality. When men touched his vagina, they were either turned off or not. True bi-sexuals enjoyed Terry in all ways possible. Homosexuals were repulsed, or not interested when they realized he had a vagina. This was true of Jami as well. Although surgery created beautiful, huge breasts, "she" retained the penis with which "she" was born. "She," too, called herself a "test" for bi-sexuality. The bi-sexual man Jamie married told me, "I am so fortunate. I found the best of both worlds – big breasts and a big penis. What more could I ask for?"

In class, I saw first hand that group sex, and the non-committed sex which was prevalent at the school, was only momentarily pleasurable. I also saw the pain of disconnection, the sadness of alienation, and the emptiness of an orgasm without an emotional connection. After witnessing all of this, however non-judgmental I am as a sex therapist, I know in my heart, and share my convictions with my clients, that sex is meant to be connected to love. Searching for the combination is more important than seeking empty sexual pleasures.

In "The Fuck-o-rama" class, I learned that however open and accessible I must be to my clients, I must also maintain my own morality, and my own belief systems. I think that throughout the years, my convictions and assessments of certain behaviors have benefited rather than hurt, anyone who has sought my advice.

CHAPTER TWO

The
Clients

MARYANN AND BURT

Maryann could not control her sobs. Nose running, eyes tearing, she told me her story in a choking, hesitant voice. "I saw Burt in the bathroom. He was wearing my bra, with paper kind of stuffed in it and was putting on lipstick, but it was really smeared, grotesque looking. Mascara was on his cheeks, smeared and running and he was masturbating with his left hand."

"How did he look?" I asked. "Did he have a happy look?"

Maryann looked at me, surprised. "What difference does it matter if he looked happy. It's disgusting! I can't even think about it," she said as her voice became stronger mirroring her upset.

"If he is happy doing something, can you accept it?" Her sobbing stopped, as she angrily responded, "No, I can't, if something disgusting makes him happy, then to hell with him."

Saying nothing, I allowed her to calm down. Finally she asked, "Why can't he be happy with something more acceptable, something other than my underwear and makeup?"

Again, I sat silently, allowing her to think about what she'd said. In any therapy, it is true that the client knows what he/she must do, wants to do, can do. If the therapist allows the silence, the answers will come without too much trouble.

Suddenly, Maryann began to giggle. Wiping her eyes, she asked, "Do you mean that if he's happy, why am I so upset?"

I walked around to her chair and asked her to stand up so that I could hug her, confirming that she'd had an AHA EXPERIENCE. This is the moment in therapy that all therapists and patients pray for; it is the moment in which everything is completely understood. And, with this understanding, there is success. The AHA is a wonderful moment. Maryann had found her own answer.

We continued to meet several more times, with Burt joining us for the remaining sessions. Maryann explained to him that she'd thought his behavior was totally disgusting, but that she did love him, and was trying to understand this "weird thing" that made him happy. She admitted to Burt,

"When I saw you I was appalled, but at the same time, I noticed what a serene, really open look you had. It was a look I hadn't seen in a long time. When Carole asked me if you looked happy, I realized that you looked more than happy; you looked peaceful."

Burt said that he had always loved silk next to his body and that it made him feel rich. He told us, "Silk is royalty; it's money and success, and it's warm and soft. I love how I feel when I rub my body with it. I love paying attention to myself by applying makeup, looking in the mirror, watching my face, my eyes, my mouth. I watched my mother applying her makeup, and I envied how happy she looked. I thought to myself, even as a small boy, that when you pay that much attention to yourself, you must really love yourself. I began playing with her makeup and felt a sense of pride that I was taking such care, paying such attention to myself. From then on, it was always a turn-on kind of ritual that I went through as sort of foreplay before I masturbated."

Maryann had a frightened look on her face as she asked, "Do you need that, even with me? Don't I turn you on, aren't I enough?" Her voice caught and she began to cry.

Burt burst into racking sobs, his body heaving. He held her and they both cried. When they calmed themselves, I explained that a fetish such as Burt had, had nothing to do with his love and passion and feelings for her. It was not mutually exclusive, but rather inclusive, if both partners could accept it. Burt's love for Maryann and his passion for her was not diminished because he enjoyed silk and makeup. In fact, it was enhanced when he was able to go through his "ritual" prior to lovemaking. "Think of it this way," I said. "If you loved a certain perfume, or incense, or candle aroma, and enjoyed using it during your lovemaking, do you think your partner would object?" Turning to Maryann I asked, "If Burt was really turned on by pink underwear or a black nightgown, would you wear it for him? What if Burt wanted to use baby powder so that his body was smooth and smelled good like he did when he was a baby — would you object to that?"

I allowed her to think about it for awhile. Maryann finally asked, "Isn't there a big difference between pink underwear on me and makeup on him?"

"Why?" I asked. After a few moments, Burt responded, "You know, that's a good question. Why is one preference better or worse than another preference, or, as you said, fetish?"

Although I no longer meet with them, Maryann and Burt, who have presently been married for 16 years, call from time to time to update me on how they are both accepting of each others pleasures. Maryann has involved herself in Burt's fetish by buying him silk underwear and teaching him how to apply makeup more efficiently. During one phone conversation, she told me, "I actually love the touch of his padded bra against me. He uses foam rubber now, not paper. I even like to wrap his silk pajamas around me. It's like being in a cocoon, wrapped in smoothness and comfort."

How different these two could have reacted. Maryann had been prepared to go directly to a lawyer and insist on a divorce from "that sick bastard." Information, non-judgmentalism, acceptance, and, of course, love, helped them through their crisis.

My original question to Maryann about how he looked was essential. She needed to stop thinking about her own feelings of disgust and pain and start thinking about the feelings of her husband. A bit of empathy is wonderful. It acts like glue and will bring a couple together very quickly if there is love and strength in the relationship. As soon as she was able to recognize that Burt was actually happy, she saw the entire situation in a different light.

REMEMBER:

If there is someone in your life who is truly happy with a behavior, think of it from his or her point of view, not from your own. And, if possible, find a way to fit it into your life, or, at the very least, allow it to remain in their's.

JULIA AND TIM

Julia entered my office with a crash, a real one. She threw the door open with such force, it hit a vase on a table behind the door. When the vase hit the wall, breaking into many small pieces, her reaction surprised me — she laughed. Julia also apologized and offered to pay for the vase, but I refused. After all, it was an accident. That is when Julia said, "You know, this is not unusual for me. I seem to be very wild, and have a lot of these small "accidents." As a therapist, I'm trained to listen for tone, sequence, attitude, etc. Julia's tone was quite pronounced. I immediately inquired about the word "wild," which she emphasized rather strongly.

Julia's face seemed to crack before me. Her beautiful mouth and full lips squeezed together into a barely perceptible line of red. Her eyes, which I'd noticed were truly

21

green, almost disappeared into a patch of eyelash and wrinkled skin. She held her long, very thick red hair in both hands and pulled through it as if trying to remove a wig. No sounds or movement other than the tightness of her body and the upward thrust of her hands in her hair came.

I had difficulty not going to her, I could feel the intensity of her pain, but I knew that any intrusion on my part at that moment, however well meaning, would be very destructive. Julia had to direct this meeting, not me. I waited. Minutes of silence passed before a sharp cry came from her. It pierced the air and sent a shiver down my spine. Julia threw her head back and said, as she released her hair, "I've reached the end. I'm going to get myself killed by someone, which is the same as doing it myself." Julia, looking very beautiful, was again in total control as she began her story. Her voice was monotone, almost inaudible, but steady and firm. It seemed as though she was telling a story about someone else, something she'd read or seen in a movie. There was no apparent emotional connection from the tale she told to her own life.

"I am not just wild," she said. "I am really a lion in a human's body. I need to be a lion; there is no other body in which I can be what is inside of me. Sometimes I go out to the country, and I can let it all out, but I need to be a lion with another lion. I need the contact, but don't know how I can have it. I try to pretend, but I can't pretend with Tim; he would not understand and would be afraid of me. So, I pick up men. And, when we get into the hotel room, I let it all out. After we have sex and I go home, I feel better, but I also feel so guilty. The sex is always great — wild like me. Once someone actually walked out of the room; I think I scared him to death. The problem is, I love Tim and know that one of these days I'll get AIDS or some guy will kill me. Most of the guys get very crazed. It frightens me, but it excites me so much, I don't know what to do," Julia finished. Her voice and expression never changed as she told me all this; she had disconnected herself from all emotion.

"Show me what you do," I said. Although I told her I wouldn't judge her, she didn't believe me.

"You'll call the men in white and have me put away," she said. "Don't say you won't judge me, you'll hate me."

Trust is very important in a therapeutic situation. The client puts all of their feelings onto the therapist if there is trust. When the therapist accepts what the client is feeling and needing, the client begins to accept it in themselves as well. This is called transference, an absolute necessity in any successful therapy.

I had to establish an atmosphere of trust for Julia so that transference could occur. I knew that nothing she could do would shock or upset me and that she was basically a normal, good person with an unusual behavior pattern. Although I also knew this behavior could become destructive if not channeled more safely, I did not even think of "curing" her or "changing" her; it was essential for me to accept her so that she could learn to accept herself. In Julia's case, it was her feelings of guilt and fear which had to be changed by channeling the behavior, not judging it or trying to stop it.

I waited quietly as Julia stared at me. She looked like she was deciding on whether or not to take a chance with me. I forced myself to show no emotion, no expression. Watching Julia carefully, I knew that my eye contact and calmness was reassuring, actually winning her confidence.

I heard the sounds for a long while before she made any expression, or movement, only sounds of purring, louder and louder.

Eventually, Julia began to growl in a muffled, low voice, her lips closed tightly, like a ventriloquist. They were sounds without movement, sounds without expression. She finally began tossing her head back, her long hair flopping against her shoulders, one side then the other. She added her arms, her hands thrusting towards me, and long fingernails threateningly near my face as she leaned forward. She stood as her growls grew louder and her expression more menacing. Her body moved in a rolling rock forward and back, her head side to side, her arms jutting forward and back. I watched carefully, trying to see how she felt about what she was doing.

It was clear that Julia was in a kind of trance within the first 30 or 40 seconds of her behavior. Her eyes rolled up, the whites showing beneath her pupils. Her movements were mellifluous, not strained or awkward at all. Her face, though distorted into an angry growling look, was expectant, passionate, full of a sense of pleasure and energy. My quiet acceptance encouraged Julia. She leaned down and began walking on her hands and feet, continuing the sounds and movements. She began whirling in circles very quickly, thrashing out at me with loud roars, her lips snarling.

Every aspect of Julia's being had become a "lion." She had indeed been transported into the jungle, into a wild and passionate being, experiencing herself as completely as possible. It was an exciting and wondrous transformation to watch. Julia lay down on her back, her hands clawing at the rug beneath her, her chest heaving in exhaustion.

I sat next to her and stroked her forehead, wiping her sweat with a tissue. As I stroked her arms, and began slowly to massage her hands, my non-verbal communication told her, "You're OK and I'm OK. I accept you, so you can accept yourself."

Paying positive attention to a client after they have shown you the piece of themselves they are uncomfortable with, is absolutely essential. Paying attention, which is accepting and validating of this piece is crucial.

In order to behave in ways that we think inappropriate or unacceptable, we often wear a mask, kind of a masquerade, so that what we are doing is not truly from ourselves but from this masked impersonator. A good example of this is the way we change our voice to a baby voice when we say loving and affectionate words such as "I luv ou so much poochhie poo." The voice allows us to be loving if we are uncomfortable with this kind of behavior. Many of us do this because we are uncomfortable. Think about when you've used a baby voice or a deeper voice, or assumed different posture to make an uncomfortable point.

Julia needed the "lion's mask or persona" in order to be a passionate, uninhibited sexual person. She felt uncomfortable with being aggressive and wild sexually. As a "lion" though, she was able to let herself go. In many ways, this was very healthy, in that she could express her sexual needs, without compromising her inherent shyness and discomfort with this aspect of herself. She did, however, learn to incorporate and accept all of herself, realizing what she'd

25

been doing was merely a temporary solution, more like a band-aid for something which was not sore.

Julia rose and walked back to her chair smiling and said, "Well, I guess you don't think I'm nuts do you?"

"No, I don't think you're nuts. I think you are passionate and creative and dramatic and wonderful," I answered, deliberately attributing labels to her actions. Creative and dramatic are socially acceptable, positive labels. After all, our famous heroes are writers and artists, and actors and athletes — all creative, dramatic, and wonderful. Part of my establishing an atmosphere of trust depended on Julia knowing how I felt and what I thought of her behavior. Giving these attributes, helped Julia to trust and to continue her therapy.

Julia came to see me twice more before she agreed to bring Tim with her for a joint session. As planned, I saw Tim alone, and explained that Julia was "dramatic and creative" and wanted to share her fantasies and her passionate "play acting" with him. Tim seemed thrilled.

"If Julia wants this, I do too," he said. "I've always told her that spicing up our sex life in any way she wanted to would be OK with me."

I explained that it was a bit unusual, and perhaps even shocking. I explained how important it was that he didn't judge Julia's ideas, or refuse to at least try "becoming part of her show." Then it was Julia's turn. She didn't show any of her "lion act." She told Tim about it.

"I like to pretend that I'm a lion. I like to growl, and prance, and threaten, pretending to scratch and maul and bite. I like to act really wild and animal-like." Tim said nothing as we all looked at each other. I had warned Julia that whatever Tim's reaction was, she had to realize and accept that it was for his own reasons, for himself, not against her. I told Julia that it would be her responsibility to allow Tim to pace himself and to allow him time as she explained herself to him. Julia accepted the challenge. It was obvious that Tim was wondering what to do and was at a loss for words. Julia accepted his reticence and discomfort.

"I know you are not discrediting my ideas and that you just don't know what I want from you," she told him. "What I want, is to go home, get into bed, and see what happens. If I feel like putting on my "lion's hat," I will. If I do, I want you to just be there for me. If it is too much for you, stop me. If it is not, maybe I can be a "lion" once in a while, and you can be my mate," Julie said before she suprisingly broke down and began to cry. It was the first time she had ever cried, despite all of the trauma and pain she'd been through with me. Tim jumped to her, pulled her from her chair and murmured words I couldn't hear, but could tell were intimate, to her. I watched their bodies merging into each other, trying to flow into a oneness, without separation. It was a profound and beautiful experience for all of us, but especially for them. Julia was as normal as most people. In fact, she was probably healthier in that she knew what excited and pleased her, and was willing to take the risks necessary for pleasure. Needless to say, it was unnecessary for Tim to know about Julia's one night stands. There was no need for that. They both knew that passion for one partner could either be passion for the other or the end of the relationship. Tim chose passion for both. They are now reaping the rewards of Julia's "wild" sexuality, and Tim's choice to share it with her.

JANET AND GREGG

Janet and Gregg were an extremely handsome couple. They looked like models, even movie stars. Sophisticated and extremely bright, they were perfect candidates for therapy. All research indicates that intelligence, as well as motivation has a great deal to do with success in therapy.

Janet had been referred to me by her gynecologist. She suffered from vaginismus, an involuntary spasm of the sphincter muscles surrounding the vaginal entrance. It is absolutely impossible to enter the vagina of a woman with this condition. In fact, vaginal examinations have to be performed under anesthesia, it is so painful. It is a devastating condition for a couple, not just for the female. Imagine attempting intercourse again and again, finding no entry, no place for insertion of a penis? Imagine how frightened, angry, frustrated and inadequate you would feel? To make matters worse, Janet and Gregg had experienced very satisfying and frequent sex for the three years of their marriage prior to this situation.

They had researched the situation, and came in to my office with their own agenda. Gregg believed that Janet's vaginismus was caused by her ambivalence about their having to move to England.

Gregg told me, "I've gotten a Rhodes Scholarship and we are planning to leave for England in September. Janet has changed her studies twice before for me, when we moved from Stanford, and when we moved here to Columbia. This will be the third time. Each time Janet has lost some of her own credits in the transfer from school to school. I know that vaginismus is caused by anger, even hatred. I know that Janet loves me and I love her, but her anger is real and well founded. My career always seems to come first. I don't want to make these changes, but the opportunities are so good." He added, "Janet even agrees," just before she interrupted him.

I had been watching her very carefully, hoping that she would interject. It is difficult to work with a couple and watch one take charge of the session. Some therapists feel that penis envy and a deep hatred of men are often involved in the dysfunction Janet was experiencing. Others believe that it is associated with fear of penetration, or even pain during attempts at penetration.

"I don't hate men, and I certainly don't hate Gregg," Janet said when she cut in on Gregg. "I wanted to tell you myself that I do agree with Gregg about my being more angry about moving than I may have even realized. We've tried everything; nothing seems to work."

Janet was very distraught. Tearful and clutching at Gregg, she turned to him and asked, "Do you still love me, because if you don't we will never get through this." Gregg held Janet very closely, stroking her hair, looking into her face, as he responded, "I love you very much, don't ever think that I don't; I'll always love you, no matter what." He turned to me and added, "Doc, if we never have intercourse again, it will be alright with me."

A red flag went up in my brain. If he didn't care, then why was he here? Why did he begin talking; why was it he who stressed how Janet's anger had probably caused this? In therapy, if a patient makes an emphatic statement such as

Gregg's, the therapist has to look at the exact opposite. It seemed especially true in this instance. Janet had only asked the question, "Do you love me?" Gregg had offered an additional answer to his reassurances.

I knew then that my direction had to be to effect a full cure and to help them to overcome whatever barriers between them created this drastic change in their previously satisfactory sex life. Janet and Gregg worked for three weeks in the regular procedures to overcome this dysfunction. Using plastic catheters of graduated thicknesses, Janet tried inserting them into her vagina. She was desensitizing herself to vaginal penetration as well as slowly relaxing the spasm of the sphincter muscle. They had oral sex, cunnilingus, as well as fellatio, and Janet was able to climax during these times. Although penetration was painful, she was gradually able to insert the most narrow of the catheters into the entrance of her vagina. They massaged each other, bathed together, brushed each other's hair, and in general were very loving and caring towards each other. They followed all of the homework and all of the procedures faithfully.

But Gregg was increasingly frustrated and his feelings of rejection were strong, despite Janet's reassurances. It was the middle of July, and time was of the essence. September was the deadline for England, and Janet had not yet decided whether or not she would go with Gregg. They discussed her staying at Columbia for another two years to finish her degree, following him at that time. Gregg took this plan as further rejection of him as Janet tried to reassure him, "We can see each other on holidays, and I'll spend each summer with you." At this point, I decided to take a risk and try what I like to call "an ax between the eyes." This "ax" is a statement which shocks the clients, but helps them to see a situation more clearly and more immediately.

As Janet was willing to offer Gregg the choice to go to England alone, I decided to suggest another choice. I said, very slowly, watching their expressions very carefully, "Why not allow Gregg to have intercourse with other women. He loves you and would never have any real relationship with anyone else. But since intercourse is lacking in your present relationship, perhaps "using" another woman for JUST this, would relieve you of your guilt feelings and give Gregg an outlet for his frustrations."

Janet's reaction was exactly as I'd hoped. She became furious at me, shouting, "You are the most unethical, unprofessional therapist I've ever heard of! How dare you tell my husband to go out and fuck someone else, how dare you!" She was practically frothing at the mouth.

Gregg, on the other hand, was very quiet. He touched Janet's arm, and said to me, "Janet didn't mean to insult you like that, I'm sure you had a reason to suggest that. Maybe you could explain it to us." Gregg was obviously interested in the idea. He had said several times during the past weeks that he missed intercourse; he wanted the connection and the feelings of warmth and closeness that only intercourse gave him. He expressed feelings of rejection because Janet remained closed to him and was desperate and frustrated enough to hope my suggestion had some credibility, some purpose. I, on the other hand, hoped he would reject this idea without any question, even become as angry as Janet had.

There was still time. He hadn't exactly said that he wanted to go with other women. I still had hope that my "ax" would work. I turned to Janet saying, "Did I shock you? Why? Your husband is a normal male, he wants penetration; he has told you he needs penetration. What would you suggest he do?" I wanted Janet to think about this, to see it from Gregg's point of view. I hoped her empathy for his situation would mollify some of the anger she felt as she was forced to move again.

Janet cried, "It's not my fault. I don't know why this happened. You can't blame me, it's not fair."

"No one is to blame," I said, "That's not the point. While you and Gregg are solving these problems, and you're doing very well I might add, why not allow him some relief from his present feelings of frustration and rejection?"

Janet began to think I had a valid professional reason for continuing this line of discussion. She turned to Gregg and asked him, "If she's serious, and it's an alright thing for you to do, would you want to do it?"

I held my breath. This was truly a crucial moment. Gregg's reaction was the key to Janet's releasing her anger or reinforcing it.

"I was wondering why she said that," he said. "To tell you the truth, for a minute there, I did want to hear more about it. But the way you just looked at me, with so much love, I know that I could never, ever, touch another woman, ever. I never want you to be afraid of that again. I never want to see fear in your face, I only want to see love."

His response was perfect. Janet melted into his arms. I left the room for a few moments. They needed to be alone and to realize what had happened. When threatened with this untenable, but possible alternative to their situation, they both clung together, frightened by that possibility. Realizing how much she loved Gregg, and how much he loved her, Janet released her need to finish her degree at Columbia.

Instead, she looked forward to two years in a foreign country. They continued their therapy for two more weeks with complete success. The "ax" had worked.

Sometimes there are secondary gains which are achieved with a psychological dysfunction such as this. Janet was able to punish Gregg, even though it wasn't what she really wanted. If the punishment meant she might lose him, or he might be unfaithful to her, she'd rather let go of it. Although her motivations were unconscious, her awareness of all of the possible ramifications of vaginismus were stronger than her unconscious motivations. It was also essential that Gregg responded as he did — he reaffirmed that he truly loved her, and that he, too, was willing to make "sacrifices," as he was asking her to make for him. His statement actually told her, I'll give up penetration for you. It made her much more willing and able to temporarily give up her education for him.

At their "going-away" party, Janet hugged and thanked me. She confided that they had 'partial' intercourse. "I'm still very tight inside and out," she told me, "but I am open and we are going to have a ball in England. Thank you."

BOB AND LILLIAN

Lillian had encouraged Bob to be a sexual explorer. She told him, "Take risks, try new things, be inventive." She was most interested in exploring in the direction of control and power, known as sexual bondage.

When Bob came for an appointment with me, he explained that his sexual life had gotten out of control. He told me he needed to talk, to get advice, and to get off the destructive roller coaster he'd been on. He sat in the huge brown velvet armchair, explaining that Lillian had refused to join him for therapy. He was silent, stroking the velvet. "It's so soft," he murmured. "I like soft and gentle and I don't know how all this happened to me."

In the silence that followed, I sat patiently, allowing Bob to find his own rhythm. I did not want to break the moment for him, change it in ways he might not want, in ways which might destroy any chance of his opening up to me, by speaking.

"Lillian likes to be taken care of," he finally said. She likes to be childlike and helpless. I take care of the money, the details, and remind her of appointments. I'm there all the time so that she doesn't feel alone. If I'm not there, she says she'll just fall apart."

When I hear this kind of description, I know that Lillian is probably the stronger of the two. She is doing the controlling. Helplessness is very powerful. It makes some people feel strong and needed. Bob was one of these people. Lillian had him just where she wanted him by playing the "little girl." I also thought that she probably had some trauma in her own life, which precipitated her need to "be controlled."

The interesting factor in situations like this is that the "helpless" partner is usually quite successful and self-sufficient outside of the relationship. This proved to be true in Lillian's case. She was a successful real estate agent who knew how to run her career, but, who at home, couldn't remember her own sister's phone number. When she asked Bob, it never occurred to him that she was being manipulative. He enjoyed taking care of her, and the feeling that she needed him, but the kind of caretaking Lillian wanted had finally become unacceptable to him. He sat before me, desperate and frightened. He pulled at his collar frequently, wiped his forehead and face, bit his nails, and seemed to rock in the huge chair, as he spoke. Although his rugged features and body projected an outdoors model type, his words and demeanor were that of a little boy.

"At first it was kind of fun," he told me. "I would tie her with a scarf or something, and she'd say how excited she was because she knew I was in control, and she was totally helpless. Then she wanted me to, as she said, take more control. She bought handcuffs, and had me cuff her to the water pipe in the tub, the headboard, even the doorknob in the bedroom. She would beg for sex, and if I wanted to make love to her before she begged for it, she wouldn't let me. She wanted me to tease her and tell her she was being punished. She told me not to kiss her or do anything to her until she was screaming for it. And you know, no matter how much she screamed, when I would try to take her in my arms, she'd push me away, and say it was 'too soon – punish me, punish me.' It eventually worsened. Lillian wanted me to hit her, actually hit her. She bought a whip that was kind of soft velvet or cotton. But it hurt; I know it did. She insisted, screamed for it, again and again. I don't know how it happened, but now I'm really into it. I hit her really hard, and she seems to be having an orgasm. I leave her tied up screaming for an hour, sometimes more, before I go back to her, and then we finally make love. The worst part is that it is really very passionate, wild sex. I feel out of control and scared. It bothers me that I feel good when I hit her and make her scream. How did I get this way? How could this have happened to us? I know it's sick, and getting worse. When I saw you on TV, I thought maybe you would be the one to help me, to help us."

Bob was very still suddenly, waiting as though my response was his very lifeline to safety, a return to normalcy, as he put it.

"Tell me how I can go back to sex, and love, and Lillian, without all of this craziness!"

If you ever decide to try bondage as part of your sex life, be forewarned that it is very seductive. Being in control of someone who is tied offers a sense of power which we don't ordinarily feel in our lives. It can be exhilarating. As a result, it is sexually stimulating, and passionate. In the same way being controlled is often very frightening, it, too, can be stimulating and sexually exciting. Think about why we go to horror movies. When we are frightened in this way, our bodies come more alive, almost energized. One of my clients told me that when he goes to see a terrifying movie, he feels "totally alive."

These feelings are dangerous since they indicate that the "real world" of day to day living is not fulfilling enough. The void some people feel is often filled in dangerous and destructive ways. Trying to fill the void can escalate as it did with Bob and Lillian. Be sure of what you are doing, and why you're doing it. It is essential that you continue to enhance your sexual experiences with creativity and passion. Too often we lose interest after years of marriage, and this need not happen. I recommend doing whatever it takes, turn-on films, cybersex, fantasy, playacting, magazines, sex tools, etc. BUT, and it's a very big BUT — know what you are into and know if it is getting out of control. Bob knew, and seeking therapy was absolutely essential for him.

Lillian came to see me two weeks later. She denied having any problems with their sexual choices and insisted that she loved every minute of it, and that if Bob didn't want to continue, she would be turned off permanently.

"I need the stimulation of what you call bondage. I like it and I want it," Lillian said acting very tough as she strode around the room. I don't allow smoking but I could see her as Bette Davis, cigarette swinging and hips rotating. I could see that Lillian's defense mechanisms were tightly wrapped around her, protecting a part of her that was very fragile and decided to use my "ax" technique.

"What did he do to you, and when did it happen?" I asked very quietly, almost in a whisper. I intuitively felt that Lillian needed to re-live something in the past that terrified, yet excited her, something she couldn't understand or accept. I wasn't sure if she even remembered what it was, but I was sure something had happened.

"Who are you talking about, what in hell are you talking about?" She stared at me, shoulders hunched forward, her hands on her hips, her eyes glaring. "You damn well better explain what you're talking about."

"Lillian," I said quietly, while standing up and moving in front of her. I felt she might need to reach out to me, to be able to contact me physically if she did begin to tell me the truth. Whatever it was, I knew it was painful, something she felt she needed to be punished for, something which she was reliving now with Bob.

"Lillian, when a woman wants to be controlled, to be hurt, and to be punished as you do, I believe that she has a similar experience in her past. I believe you did not begin to want and need to behave in these ways without some cause.

37

You can trust me with it, you can tell me about it."

She stood there silently, expressionless and unmoving; she seemed frozen. I began to worry if I pushed her too hard. Was my "ax" being destructive rather than constructive? "Lillian," I continued, "it is important that we have as much information as possible, so that the problems you and Bob are experiencing can be solved. We can work together so that you and Bob can begin again, he loves you so much."

Lillian began to sob, deep wrenching sounds which shook her body in violent spasms. I didn't move. I couldn't interrupt her breakthrough. Her entire defense mechanism was being released. Anything I did would interrupt that flow and she needed to get it out, to free herself of it. Lillian cried for minutes, although it seemed like hours, before finally reaching out to me. We held on to each other for a long time. I eased her into the big comfortable armchair, and sat on the edge holding her hands in mine.

I said as gently as I could, "It was very horrible, but we can clear it out and take away the pain. We can take care of it so that it doesn't take over any more. We can give you back your power, give you back control of your life."

"How can you know that, how can you be so sure, so smug? You don't even know what happened; you can't even imagine," she said, barely audible through her tears.

I took a risk again and said, "I know that something terrible happened. I know that you've been suffering with this memory and letting the memory take over; I know that you can't go on this way; and I know that we must take away your demons."

Lillian sat back, took her hands out of mine, and told me her story. "I remember all of it, but I had no idea that it was affecting me this way. I thought I had put it behind me. Bob and I have been married six years. I started insisting we experiment after the first year, in which we were pretty normal I guess, although I have to admit I was also pretty bored. I wasn't that passionate, and was very seldom satisfied. When I asked Bob to pretend to tie me, it was on a whim. I had not thought of my dad for years. I did not know it was connected. But our sex was great and wild with passion, I wanted more and more. It was as though a scarf wasn't enough, or make believe wasn't enough. I had to really be totally helpless, unable to move my arms, unable to get out of the knots or the cuffs. That's when the need for pain began. That, too, turned me on and made me wilder and wilder. Every orgasm was an explosion deep within me. I began to experience my orgasms as a kind of cleansing of my past. I felt that I deserved to feel this good, no matter what the price, the pain or the humiliation. It was worth it because I would feel so good. When you spoke just now, I realized that I felt that way as a child. When my father would abuse me, I would be in agony sometimes, ashamed and mortified, but my body felt good. He gave me so much physical pleasure along with the agony. I've been playing out my childhood with Bob, turning him into my father, needing the pleasure regardless of the price."

I asked Lillian to show me a scene from her childhood. I wanted her to not only talk about it, but to re-live it, so she could experience an emotional catharsis during the playacting. It was a very difficult task for her, but I believe she understood the need for her body to remember as well as her mind. Because memories are stored in every area of our bodies, by putting ourselves in similar physical positions, the memory of the moment is enhanced. Re-living a situation is always more intense and therefore more helpful than merely talking about it. Because Lillian was already feeling better, she trusted that my request was logical.

Lillian dropped to the floor. She knelt, holding my knees in her hands. She put her head to the floor and began rocking back and forth. She said, "He would tie me so that I had to lean on my knees. I could only move back and forth a little. I couldn't get up or I would choke on the rope around my neck. If I cried or made any sounds, he would tighten the ropes on me. Then he would begin to penetrate me anally. He would play with my clitoris as he fucked me, and when he came into me, he'd untie me, and begin to stroke me so lovingly, and then he'd begin to eat me. I would have one orgasm after the other. Imagine lying on a basement floor, cold tile under me, and I'd be in ecstasy, even though my own father was the one making the bells ring."

Lillian smirked and shrugged her shoulders, "Sick huh, I know I'm really sick — but that's what happened. I thought, well I'm grown-up now, I'm a survivor as they say — I'm not a victim. I'll be OK, and I thought I was, until now."

"You are not sick, and yes, you are a survivor," I told her. "It is inconceivable that you survived such torture and humiliation from such a demented, cruel person. It is a testimony to you, to your intelligence and your emotional strength that you have survived and succeeded as you have. You have a man who loves YOU, who wants to take care of YOU. You are successful in your career, and you are emotionally healthy — you are here working on yourself, realizing you need help, and that is your strength, not your weakness. And most important of all, you have so much love inside of you. Your love for Bob is the road which will take you to complete success."

I don't usually say as much as I did this time, but Lillian kept looking at me, waiting for more reassurance, expecting me to put more and more support systems under her trembling psyche.

"He was sick Lillian, very, very sick," I added. You survived him, you conquered him, and now you'll conquer that small part of him that is still within you. I promise you - you will win."

Lillian shared her story with Bob. More importantly, she confronted her father. She needed him to apologize to her, to free her of any misguided feelings of responsibility. When Lillian and Bob confronted him, he denied everything at first. Lillian told me that she lost control, smacked him across the face and kicked him on his ankle. He went to hit her but Bob stopped his father-in-laws hand mid-air. Bob told me that he couldn't help but take over at that point, telling Joe, Lillian's father, "You are an animal. You should be in jail for the rest of your life for what you did. Lillian doesn't want revenge, she doesn't want any part of you at all — she just wants you to apologize and to admit what a pig you are. She wants to hear the words that describe what you really are, and that is what she will remember about you, nothing else, just the words admitting you are the devil incarnate, an animal who deserves to die in the cruelest and most vicious way possible. Say it, you bastard, or I'll kill you myself."

Lillian told me that she had never been as in love or proud of Bob in her life than at that moment. She knew then, that her past was really being taken care of, and that the distorted sexual games she and Bob had played were not signs of "love." As her father refused to talk and sat in stony silence, she decided right there that it was over, but that she wanted to give him a scare, something for him to suffer over, as she had suffered under his hands.

"OK you bastard, I'll see you in court," she threatened him. "I'm pressing charges against you and hope you rot in jail. And, I'm suing you for every penny you have. You're not walking away from this, not anymore." Even though Lillian knew she wasn't going to do these things, because lawyers and courts and testimony would not change anything, they would only perpetuate the pain and the horror of her childhood, she thought it would give her father a scare. We had discussed the possibility of revenge, and that it had a two edged sword. She knew she would suffer more if she continued this in any way. She wanted nothing from him, and nothing to do with him.

"You know Carole, I held my head high as I walked away from that bastard; I was full of such pride and self-respect. I have a man who loves me, and who is taking care of me in a real way, and I love myself because I have really taken care of myself. Just before Bob and I made it to the door, our hands locked together, and my father finally called out, "Forgive me, I am an animal, I am a pig. I am whatever you want to call me. But, please don't put me in jail; I'll die there."

"You know Carole," Lillian said, "when he said that, I knew he was being a real pig, just selfish and self-serving. He was pleading for himself, not trying to relieve me of any guilt, or pain, or feelings of responsibility, just hoping to stop me from telling on him. I didn't even turn around. We just walked out and closed the door very quietly. I would not give him the pleasure of showing him any anger, any feeling at all."

I asked Lillian if she had truly let go of her rage and guilt. She told me she had. Evidence for this was the new relationship she and Bob were establishing. They followed all of the homework exercises I had given them, which stressed gentle, loving, slow, behaviors. They brushed each other's hair, massaged, spoke gently and lovingly, danced together, bathed and showered, etc. And, they held a ritualistic burning of the paraphernalia which had been used in their past sexual life.

Lillian admitted, "I don't get as wild and crazily passionate, but I know what really loving someone is all about and I know that this new, gentle and loving sex is much more fulfilling for longer periods of time. Before, I would always cry after my climax. Bob could not understand and neither could I. But now I realize how much pain I was in. The physical pleasure was so full of emotional pain and those agonizing memories, that I would break down in hysterics, it wasn't really good — just wild. I want good now; I need good now — and that's what I have."

Lillian and Bob are truly OK. They worked with me for nine weeks and called from time to time afterwards to tell me how they were doing.

Lillian used Bob as a sounding board again and again, telling what her dad had done to her, and watching for Bob's reaction. Each time he was able to reassure her, to convince her of her own innocence, of her dad's total responsibility, and of his own love for her. Each of these incidents acted as steel pillars creating a stronger and stronger foundation for Lillian to stand on.

In these instances, it is important that the client actually forgives the perpetrator. Forgiveness does not mean you take them back into your life, or ever allow them access to your emotional security. It means that you let go of the anger and the pain. It means that you wipe them from your life completely, because that is what they deserve. You keep the memory safely tucked away where it has no effect on your present. Your strength sustains your feelings as positive and loving, impervious to the horror of the memory.

Lillian wrote her story in vicious detail so she and Bob could purge it from their lives. They burned the manuscript, and put the ashes into a small box which was buried in the backyard of Lillian's childhood home.

"We left it there, and it is over," she told me. "I even went to my mother's grave and told her that I forgive her, in case she knew what was going on."

I believe in rituals, I believe in actions such as Lillian's and Bob's. Your brain is imprinted with the memory of the fire, the burial, and the end of it. The ritual will be etched over and above the old memories and help you to be in control.

REMEMBER:

Childhood abuse leaves the deepest and most painful scars, but none are so deep that you can not take control of them. By telling the story, filling the scars with love and awareness, taking them out of the darkness of shame, you purge them, take control, and realize your own power.

PENNY AND CHARLES

Charles chose to sit in the ladder back chair which was in front of the window. Penny sat in a small beige armchair in front of my desk. They chose not to be near each other, and not to sit in the large brown velvet armchairs. Sitting in the large chairs could mean that they were at ease in the situation, or that they didn't mind feeling vulnerable, sunken into the huge cushions and deep seat. Or, it could mean that they were so scared they needed to lose themselves in the massive size of the chair. I tell you this because I never know why people choose the chairs they choose, or the positions they choose. I try not to jump to any conclusions. It is true that there are clues in every motion, every choice, every word, but, it is the job of the therapist to find out what the clues mean, not to conclude they are evidence. I may ask questions based on my opinion, and I may throw 'axes' based on my interpretations, but I do not assume. You know the old adage, "if you assume, you make an ass of you and me!"

Charles confirmed my first thought when he said, "We can't even sit next to each other anymore. Did you notice that? She is so mad at me all the time, I just can not take it anymore. I told Penny we should go to a lawyer or one of those divorce negotiators, not to a therapist." I waited, making eye contact with Charles, since he had spoken. I didn't want to look at Penny, which might give her the idea that I expected her to speak. Again, I have to be careful not to give clients messages which interfere with their own agenda, or lead them in any way.

45

As I expected, Charles continued, "See what I mean? Penny doesn't even talk about it. We are here to talk and I am the only one doing the talking. She is such a bitch. This is typical; everything is on me. I have to do everything, and no matter what happens, it is all my fault."

Penny turned to face Charles. "It is your fault. You are the one with the problem, not me. You are the god-damned impotent bastard, not me."

There was so much rage between these two that something had to be done immediately, or we would never succeed. I stood up, took Penny's hand, and reached across to Charles. Luckily, he responded to my gesture and took my hand as he walked towards me. I put Charles' hand on top of Penny's and said very quietly, "Do you remember your wedding day? Close your eyes and remember the day you were married."

Charles stood while Penny sat, their eyes closed and their faces softened. Charles took Penny's hand in both of his and stood there while Penny began to stroke Charles hands with her other hand. I brought the ladder back chair closer to Penny's, so Charles could sit next to her. In a few moments, he opened his eyes and sat down. They were both silent.

Bringing a joyous memory into an out of control situation works almost every time. No one can ever forget the glory of their wedding day. Even at the most painful moments, a smile will come to the mouth of someone remembering this kind of pleasure.

I continued the moment by saying, "Let's begin now, in the midst of that memory. Let's not go into the present for a while. Tell me how you met. Tell me about your wedding, your honeymoon. Let's take a journey through the past."

Animated and excited, Penny and Charles both spoke, laughing at certain recollections, even looking lovingly at each other at times, while continuing to touch each other's hands.

Penny reminded Charles of the rose petals he had put on the sheets for their first anniversary, saying how she loved his creativity and thoughtfulness. Charles reached over and touched Penny's shoulders and said, "I loved you so much then, I just couldn't get enough of you. What is happening to us? How did this happen?"

This question is relevant to so many situations. We go through life not taking control of problems or serious situations in our lives. We act as ostriches do, hiding our heads in the sand, hoping the problems will go away. But they don't, they only get worse, as Charles and Penny discovered. As their story unfolded, it became clear that there was a turning point. Neither of them realized it at the time, but the change began when Penny insisted they move to New York, so she could be closer to her aging parents.

Charles thought he was excited, even happy about the move. His company transferred him to their New York office, he and Penny's apartment was fabulous, their lifestyle was exciting and their friends stimulating and fun. He thought it was the best move they ever made and did not allow himself to realize Penny had taken control of his life, and that however OK it seemed on the surface, unconsciously, he resented the control she had exercised over him.

The rift began with small remarks. Charles would say that he missed his parents in Chicago, and wanted to go to visit them. He would talk to old friends for long periods of time, and if Penny interrupted these conversations in any way, he would chastise her saying, "Well, if you had not wanted to move, I would be able to see them, not just telephone."

He also began making trips to Chicago, first on the pretense of work, then to see friends or family. He tested Penny by inviting his parents to visit for a week and then insisted they stay another day, and another day, until it was a month before they left. It was very trying since he and Penny slept in the living room of their one bedroom apartment. Charles had no idea that he was angry, and that he was trying to get back at Penny for changing their lives so drastically. Even more importantly, he took no responsibility in the fact that they made the decision jointly. After all, he did agree to move and ask for a transfer, and he did help in finding the apartment. His unconscious was working overtime, impelling him to be a "man," to take control again. He didn't know it, but he was furious with himself, not with Penny. He never wanted to move, but he agreed to it so that they wouldn't have a controversy.

Charles had always acquiesced in the name of "peace." Even as a boy, he was the arbitrator and "mature" one in the family, settling all the arguments between his two sisters, and brother. He even settled arguments between his parents, and his parents and siblings. He was a born arbitrator. He was able to ask the right questions, and find the right solutions for everyone. He had also never thought of himself as someone who 'gives in.' He always felt he had control and power through his negotiation skills. Their move to New York was not even questioned.

During our third session, he said, "I guess I knew how important it was to Penny so I said nothing. I agreed immediately, not allowing myself to even recognize that it was something I did not want to do. What I knew I did not want to do was to disappoint Penny, so I just went along with it. It was easy to be transferred to our New York office; it all seemed so simple. I didn't realize what a Pandora's Box would be opened."

As is often the case, Charles' anger manifested itself in silly unimportant ways, such as when Penny didn't pick up the laundry, or when she forgot to give him a message, or she left her stockings on the shower rack, again, etc. We all know the nitpicking that goes on when there is an underlying agenda driving the anger. If you are becoming picky, nasty, and sarcastic about small unimportant things, you may want to face the underlying cause for this anger, rather than have it inevitably mushroom into something very destructive. If a couple is not kind and respectful to each other, passion and romance are not uppermost in their minds. I tell my clients that the most stimulating sexual aphrodisiacs are the three R's — Reward, Respect, and Recognition. Imagine if your spouse is respectful all of the time, recognizes your new haircut or sweater, and rewards you by thanking you for picking up the milk or running the tub or buying the paper. When these three R's are prevalent in your daily life, sex will be, too. Without them, sex disappears in a haze of resentment and avoidance.

Penny and Charles were in that haze. Penny began rejecting Charles' infrequent sexual advances. The cause, most often, was because she had been embarrassed, criticized, or ignored by Charles five minutes before he wanted to make love. Because she was not in the mood, he felt rejected. The vicious cycle came full circle. Charles' resentment, his unconscious anger, and his destructive behavior were debilitating for both of them. Penny's understandable rejection only fueled his negative feelings. Impotence really was the easy way out. Charles no longer felt rejected, or the need to try to make love to Penny. He couldn't; he had a dysfunction. And, he told himself, it didn't matter because he didn't want to have anything to do with her anyway. Penny, on the other hand, was devastated. On the few occasions when she wanted to make love, Charles remained flaccid, unable to function. To cover his emotional pain, he appeared unconcerned about the situation.

When they came to see me, they had become aware that something had to be done. They were behaving hatefully to each other. Their constant bickering in front of their friends caused them to be avoided. Friends were telling them to get help, warning them that it looked like divorce was the best solution for their problems.

When Charles spoke about his unhappiness with their move to New York on their first visit, Penny was dumbfounded. She had no idea he not only did not love New York, but that he did not really want to move in the first place. He felt manipulated and controlled which always results in resentment and anger. Ergo, the hateful remarks, the distasteful behavior, the tension and anxiety between the two. When we don't admit our true feelings, even to ourselves, these feelings are manifested insidiously and destructively.

When Charles was able to admit that he had felt out of control ever since Penny made the decision to move, she was able to identify with his feelings and empathize with him.

"Let's go back to Chicago," she said, "I love you too much to go on with this. When friends suggested we get divorced, I almost fainted. I couldn't breathe. I can not imagine life without you. New York and my parents will get along without us. You and I are too important to let this happen."

Penny's acquiescence, admission of love, willingness to give it all up for Charles, was astonishing to him. "I thought you didn't care," he told her, "I really thought you were so involved with your job, our new friends, and your parents, that I was second, even third, in importance to you. God knows, when you considered me first, I didn't see it at all, anywhere. I can not believe you mean what you are saying."

"I'll show you I mean it," Penny responded. "Call your office right now, ask for a transfer back to Chicago, and I will quit right now, too."

Charles turned to me and said, "Doc, do you think I can get it up now that I believe Penny still loves me?"

His question brought laughter from all of us. Penny moved to Charles' side and began stroking his face, "If you can not get it up, we will still manage, and besides, who cares what Doc thinks, it is me you will be getting it up for!" Then she laughingly added "Besides, I'll have a lot of fun trying"

Again we laughed, and then got down to serious business. We knew that Charles did not have a physiological problem. He could attain an erection and climax during masturbation. Therefore, we concluded it was situational impotence. We also knew the anger had been ameliorated and that love and trust had been re-established, all good signs. But, we also knew that impotence does not just go away. I did not expect that Charles would be able to go home and make love to Penny. I also told them it would NOT be a good idea for Penny to "try to get it up, for Charles."

I suggested they follow my program faithfully, so that Charles did not experience the trauma which may arise from "SEXPECTATIONS," a word I coined meaning expectations of sexual behavior which are unrealistic.

I gave them explicit instructions, a step by step program, which they promised to follow. These steps are essential since they relieve the dysfunctional partner of any pressure. Also, and very importantly, they made contracts, which they had to abide, and which offered the message that the dysfunction is not a burden, but something which each partner is willing to accept while working towards a cure.

I — CREATE A "NON-DEMAND CONTRACT"

Penny and Charles wrote: "We will not make love, nor will we expect to climax or satisfy each other in any way. We will massage, bathe, laugh, dance, talk, and eat together, but we will not make love."

II — CREATE A "LET'S REALLY TRY CONTRACT"

"I, Penny, promise, and I, Charles, promise, that we will do everything in our power to fulfill our non-demand contract."

III — CREATE A "NON-PENETRATION CONTRACT"

"We will make love passionately and lovingly in every way other than through penetration. If I, Charles, attain an erection, I will climax through masturbation or oral sex. If I, Penny, am ready to climax, I will be satisfied with cunnilingus, fingering, or a vibrator. I will not expect, demand, or even allow penetration."

IV — CREATE A "FULL SEXUALITY CONTRACT"

(It is essential the male have an "escape clause" in this contract.)

"We will make love as we used to, completely and wildly, and whenever we both want to. If it is not mutual, we will not even begin to make love. If I, Charles, feel that I am losing my erection, I will either not penetrate at all, or pull away from Penny until I feel confident that my erection is sufficient for penetration.

I, Penny, will have no expectations if Charles wants to stop thrusting. It will be his choice, and we will continue with other oral sex or masturbation."

These contracts are followed for an indefinite period of time. When a couple feels comfortable they go on to the next contract, or the next phase of their lovemaking.   It is absolutely essential the dysfunctional partner is in full control of the contracts.

Charles and Penny were actively making love using all of their "tricks" and "joys" within two weeks. Charles took control of the timing of the contracts. He decided when HE was ready to go on to contract II, and then to III, and IV. Charles continued to masturbate to attain an erection for the first few months. Penny realized that it was Charles' call and was not offended or turned-off in any way. In fact, Penny would lick on Charles nipples, or testicles, or the tip of his penis, as he masturbated.

They tried "stuffing," which is placing the flaccid penis into the vagina. The warmth and moisture of the vagina is a turn-on, and often stimulates the male to an erect state. Many couples enjoy this, but Charles did not. He felt inadequate and embarrassed about it, so they did not use this technique as one of their "tricks." (Stuffing is an excellent technique for older men who have difficulty attaining an erection or who become partially, but not fully erect.)

Respect and love for each other which had been renewed, was the real turn-on for them. Charles felt loved by Penny's willingness to "give it all up for him" and Penny felt loved when she realized that all of the pain they had gone through was due to his unconscious, not conscious behavior.

Together they obtained success, because, they not only followed their sexual contracts, they also followed their "LOVE CONTRACT," which stated "Be honest, tell each other what is on your mind. Do not sacrifice for your partner. Always discuss issues and compromise with each other, but DO NOT SACRIFICE. Sacrifice will only result in resentment and serious problems. Compromise and discuss but don't sacrifice."

If you do something you don't want to do, it will show its ugly face in other ways. There is no free lunch, believe me. Be honest, if you don't want to see a movie, say so. If you don't want to go to dinner, say so. Disappointment once in a while is much more healthy than the kind of insidious "pay-back" which you will get if your partner sacrifices for you. Remember that and be sure when you make decisions they are truly mutual.

FOLLOW RITUALS:

Daily discussion of needs, wants, problems — EVERY DAY — at least five minutes a day.

Compliment each other — EVERY DAY — at least once. Be sincere and DO IT!

Kiss each other hello and goodbye - not a perfunctory split second peck - a real lip to lip kiss.

Kiss each other good morning and good night - EVERY DAY!

Be kind and polite, show RESPECT ALL OF THE TIME. Make believe that your partner is a stranger. Would you use that tone? Would you say those things? Would you do those things? Why do it with someone who is your life partner? Think about it. Remember the three R's of good sex: RESPECT, RECOGNITION, REWARD.

REMEMBER:

If you are among the hundreds of thousands of couples who have suffered terribly due to poor communication, hidden feelings, and general dishonesty, you don't have to be. CHANGE! JUST DO IT! Make life happen the way you want it to!

RENEE AND PAUL

Renee entered my office with a splash, literally. She was carrying a container of coffee, which spilled all over the floor as she came in. Trying to clean it up, she bent over exposing her breasts and nipples. "I'll clean that up if you can get me some tissue or something. I'm sorry about that," she apologized, as she moved toward me, swinging her hips and licking her lips. She seemed a caricature of a beautiful porno star at an audition.

"Let it go for now," I said, waiting for her to begin the session. It was HER session, and I didn't want to intrude on it in any way. Anything that I said could change her agenda, so I was silent. She continued making comments about her "accident," concentrating on the spilt coffee instead of the reason she had come.

This is known as avoidance due to discomfort on the part of the client. I allowed her to find her own time, saying nothing to her comments about the coffee. Finally, she seemed to settle down and let go of her need to avoid her own issues.

She sat quietly, stroking the inside of her wrist with her fingers. I noted the stroking, thinking she seemed to be masturbating. I wondered if she was sexually frustrated. I know it may seem an outrageous thought, but any form of repetitive touching is, in reality, masturbation.

Checking the clock on my desk, I realized that five full minutes had gone by. A knock on the door interrupted the silence, and Paul entered the room.

"I thought you weren't coming," Renee said harshly.

"I'm here, OK, do you want me to leave?"

Renee said nothing. Paul sat down and said, "Hi Dr. Altman. I'm sorry we're so angry with each other. It wasn't always like this."

As Renee's huge dark eyes filled with tears, I suddenly noticed how very beautiful, soft and fragile looking she was. There was a total transformation from her harsh, cheap looking appearance. She was a truly beautiful woman, who probably looked great in the morning.

As she looked at her husband, a man who looked like he stepped out of a magazine ad, tears flowed down her cheeks and she said, "I know, I know, I know how good it was - what changed, what is happening to us? It was so good, so perfect. What is going on?"

"The problem is you don't realize that you are walking around with your tits hanging out, your skirts up to your snatch, your tongue making gestures all the time, to anyone and everyone. You act like a slut, don't you realize that?"

Rather than allow this attack and accusatory tone to continue, I ignored Paul's hostile remarks and said to Renee,

"You're crying."

She began to sob, a reaction which I had expected. When you validate someone's feelings, the feelings are usually exacerbated, increased. By noticing her tears, she was given permission to let them out. And, as I had expected, Paul reacted. He immediately went to her, and put his arms around Renee.

"Please don't cry," he said, "I'm sorry about all of this, I just can not take it anymore, I love you so much, that is why I'm here. We will work it out, I promise."

Paul turned to me and said, more loudly and emphatically,

"We will work this out, won't we?"

When one partner, such as Renee, has a higher sex drive, the other partner feels inadequate, pressured, annoyed, even angry, like Paul. Of course, Renee felt rejected, unattractive, unloved because of Paul's frequent rejections to her sexual overtures. The goal for their therapy revolved around finding an even playing field, a place where they could both feel comfortable.

Paul needed to accept that Renee's sexuality requires more frequent satisfaction and fulfillment than his. They both had to realize that no one was at fault. There was no blame in this situation. Our sex drives develop very early in our lives, and don't change because we are in love. When we are sexually satisfied, in accordance with our personal needs, we are truly not interested, despite the possibilities presented. Renee felt that by acting like a 'sex-pot' and dressing to seduce Paul, he would be 'hot' for her. She also felt that making him jealous when other men reacted to her overt sexuality, would excite his passion more frequently. Instead, it backfired. Paul felt that her entire life centered around getting him into bed.

"Everything Renee does is directed towards my cock," he told me. "It seems the real me, my feelings, my needs, are totally out of the picture. Nothing about me seems to be important to her. I could be on crutches, or in a wheelchair or whatever, as long as my cock is out and hard; that is all that seems to matter. She doesn't notice anything else."

Renee was astounded by the way Paul felt. She never realized that he felt so depersonalized, so alienated from her in every way. It was essential that they begin a fresh understanding of their sexual needs.

They began telling each other, honestly, and completely, what they liked sexually, and how often they wanted it. They also initiated a series of conversations which brought them closer and closer to a mutual understanding. Renee agreed that she would masturbate if she felt the desire to be sexually satisfied. It was essential that Paul also agree to be with Renee during these times, so that she did not have to keep secrets, and hide her sexual needs from him. She also agreed not to blame him for not having the same needs. Paul agreed to accept that her sexual drive was higher than his, and he would respect her by helping her.

Paul and Renee now kiss and stroke each other while Renee masturbates, a mutually satisfying compromise to their situation. Often, Paul is turned on and they make love. Paul strokes Renee and watches her pleasuring herself. Sometimes he masturbates her or she uses a vibrator. Other times, she uses her own fingers.

Paul knows that he is not "sick" or "inadequate" and he knows that Renee is as healthy and as normal as he is. They both know they are different in many ways; their sexual clock is just one of the differences.

Their ability to accept each other, to compromise, to find sexual behaviors which are satisfying to BOTH of them, answered all of their problems. Incidentally, Renee called me a year after their last visit to tell me that she was pregnant. Paul was turned on more often than she was, for the first time in their nine years together. He was as understanding about her refusals, as she had become about his. Renee and Paul had a son, about whom Renee recently said, "He will know how personal and different sexual feelings are, and he will be taught to accept everyone as they are."

She said that the most important thing she will always remember from her therapy, and which she will teach her son, is when I said to her, "Remember, we do things, and behave in ways which are FOR OURSELVES, NOT AGAINST SOMEONE ELSE."

It is one of my favorite sayings, because I truly feel that if you realize this truth, you will feel rejected and angry and hurt, much less often. Usually the person does not want to hurt or reject you, they just want and need to take care of themselves. Respect them for their individual needs and desires. Don't turn against them or yourself because of their strength and assertion. When a couple has divergent sex drives, these are the essentials.

REMEMBER:

☐ Neither one of you is wrong.

☐ Neither one of you is right.

☐ Where there is love there is acceptance.

☐ Where there is acceptance, there is compromise.

☐ Tell your partner how he/she can help you to satisfy your sexual needs.

☐ Accept what your partner tells you and take part in what they need.

☐ Follow your own rhythm, giving no pressure to change, and accepting no pressure to change.

☐ Sex is not love, it is only an expression of love, which is often controlled by private and personal physiological propensities.

These propensities do not negate your love or even confirm your love — they are your reality.

If you are more interested in making love than your partner is, try to remember that it is not because you are not loved, it is because he/she has a rhythm different from yours. Of course, if there is anger and resentment, your sex lives will suffer. And, of course, if there is a lack of love, or a loss of love, your sex lives will suffer. It is essential that you discover the underlying reason for the problem, and deal with it at the appropriate level.

For Paul and Renee, the solution was simple because they did love each other, and did want to solve the problem, which created so much friction between them.

Ask questions. Discover the truth. Work from that truth. You, too, can learn, as Paul and Renee learned, to find a meeting ground, and to avoid the pain by concentrating on the love.

BILL AND SARA

It is difficult to believe that in 1976, a 40-year-old man was telling me the following story. Bill was a documentary producer, a very sophisticated, 6'2" stunning to look at, and successful professional whose career had taken him around the world for over 15 years. Sexually, though, he was incredibly ignorant.

"I was raised as a Fundamentalist," he told me. "I met my first wife at the religious college we attended. We never kissed, or danced, or even listened to music. We were married when we were 21, two days after we graduated. On our wedding night, we knew that my penis was supposed to be inserted into her vagina. With youth and love and the passion we felt, it was easy to find the right place. I lay there on top feeling good, liking it, but neither one of us knew what else to do. I bent to kiss my bride and began to slide off, extracting my penis. As I did I had a really good feeling, so I slid back, and as my penis went back in it felt even better. So I continued, off and on, kind of in and out, feeling great. "Does that feel good to you?" I asked, and Ellen, my first wife, said "Yes, is that what you're supposed to do?" Well long and sad story short, we learned about thrusting, but that's about all we learned. It was the missionary position, a few minutes of in and out, and we were both happy. At least I thought so until I married my second wife Sara.

Even in my travels, if I had affairs after Ellen died, I would do what I had always done. One time a woman tried to kiss my penis. I stopped her and was shocked. I thought there was something wrong with her. I never talked about sex to anyone, and I never allowed myself to read books or see films about it, even though I am in the film business.

So here I now am, married to a sex crazed woman who wants to try everything which is abhorrent to me. I don't think we can make it at all. I'm too set in my way of thinking and behaving."

After establishing that Bill did indeed love Sara, in every way other than sexually, we made a contract with each other. I would teach them how to establish their sexual practices in a way which would be comfortable and satisfying for both of them. Sara and Bill would follow the step by step program religiously and diligently.

We began the desensitization process necessary for Bill to be able to accept various sexual practices.

1. *Bill accepted Sara's kissing his knees while touching his penis.*
2. *He accepted kisses on his thigh.*
3. *He accepted kisses on his belly button.*
4. *He accepted kisses on his flaccid penis, just the tip, then along the sides.*
5. *He accepted kisses on his erect penis.*
6. *He accepted Sara taking the tip of his penis into her mouth, and eventually the entire penis into her mouth.*

During this process, they took one small step at a time. Bill had learned the relaxation technique of deep breathing and concentration. It is a simple technique.

1. *Breathe in very deeply, allowing your stomach to extend. Hold the breath, pretending that it is circling between your eyes for a moment.*
2. *Expel the breath again very deeply, pulling your stomach in, pretending to pull your belly button towards your spine. (This pushes more air out of your lungs, rids the body of carbon dioxide, and is very relaxing and energizing.)*
3. *Keep your mind on your breathing. Concentrate. Breathe in, pushing your stomach out. Hold, circling air between your eyes. Breathe out, pulling your stomach in. Relax. Concentrate.*

REMEMBER: Keep your tongue in its "secret" pocket. (Place your tongue at the very roof of your mouth and you will find an indentation which is especially made to hold your tongue in a relaxed mode, rather than being held rigidly against your teeth as most of us do.)

Bill continued concentrating on the breathing and his feelings of passionate arousal. If negative feelings or sounds of his childhood imposed themselves on him, he pushed them away. Breathe, breathe, breathe, were the words he used to drum away his mother's voice, and the voice of the "hellfire and damnation" preacher of his childhood church.

By keeping himself in the present, feeling the physical pleasures without negative thoughts or fears of punishment, he was able to allow Sara's pleasuring. As time went on, he not only "allowed" her to pleasure him, he began to enjoy the sensations intensely. All of the negatives were pushed away completely and his natural sexual being took over.

Sara was a wonderful patient. Her love was so deep, she was tuned in to Bill's emotional state so well, that she timed her behavior perfectly. She followed the desensitization program, respecting his reactions and needs. After two weeks, Bill was able to fully enjoy oral sex.

"Once in a while, he admitted, "an ugly old taboo would raise its head, but the feeling was so delicious, it overpowered my old prohibitions."

At this point, we began focusing on Sara; it was her turn. She wanted a complete sexual life with Bill and wanted him to love making love to her as completely as she wanted to make love to him. He began learning how to satisfy Sara's needs.

1. *Bill initiated the desensitization process by kissing parts of her body with which he was comfortable. He kissed her breasts, and after a while was able to suck on her nipples. Although Bill had often thought of suckling Sara's breasts, he was unable to. He thought himself crazy for even thinking about doing such a thing.*
2. *He kissed her knees, even her toes. Then he kissed her inner thighs and her pubic mound. (He was merely brushing his lips on top of the various areas of Sara's skin.)*
3. *He lightly kissed her clitoris, still merely brushing his lips along her skin.*
4. *Bill continued to take deep breaths, and concentrate on his own passion, and Sara's pleasure. He pushed away any negative feelings or thoughts by concentrating on his breathing and his physical pleasure as he was being desensitized.*
5. *Sara made no demands and did not push or question anything. They acted slowly and carefully, making love in comfortable ways after their practice exercises, so that neither one was frustrated.*

Bill told Sara during one of our last sessions, "I get so excited with all of these new things, that I don't even think about it, it's as though my body is in total control. My mind is not as much a part of it as it used to be. You drive me wild enough to drive out all the old wives tales of hell and punishment."

The sex drive, and the natural sexual response is so powerful that if you give it a chance, it will indeed take over. Try new techniques, new positions, new ways of kissing and licking. Try them slowly and use the desensitization technique of getting closer and closer to the desired place and the desired act. Allow your passion and your love for each other to take over. If it is not for you, don't push yourself. Try something else. You never can tell — you might just find the kind of passion and pleasure you never even imagined possible.

Bill and Sara are still experimenting. Bill says his only regret is that he wasted so many years. In response to this, I told him, "Never look back, there is only NOW, and NOW you are taking care of yourself, instead of depriving yourself; that is what is important. Today is the first day of the rest of your lives. Enjoy every moment."

REMEMBER:

Life is a smorgasbord, and most of us are so inhibited, so repressed, so non-adventurous and creative, that we are at this incredibly sumptuous banquet of life, but we are starving to death. Isn't that sad? You can change it! Take the big bites out of life! Make life happen!

ROB AND JOAN

When Rob was about three years old, he was sitting on the top step, able to see his mother's legs as she put on her stockings in the upstairs bathroom. At that moment, he became aware of an erection and the pleasure that the erection gave him. From that point on, Rob's turn-on cue for sexual arousal was a woman's legs in stockings.

66

He loved stockinged legs and every woman he saw who was wearing stockings. If a 90-year-old walked in front of him wearing stockings, he would feel a stir. If he was in a lingerie shop, he'd go straight for the stocking display, while his wife Joan shopped. He loved to wear stockings himself, the feel of them stirred him, and the touch of them against Joan's skin drove him wild. He even liked to hold stockings in his hands while making love, fondling Joan with his stockinged hands.

Joan's love for Rob was the motivation for accepting all of this behavior, even though she always thought he was "sick" and that she must be "sick" too, for allowing him to do these things. Because her fears of being this way began to fester, she began to resent his behavior and feel inadequate because she "wasn't enough for him." She also became turned off by his sexual approaches, which was something that had never happened in the five years they had been married.

They came to me confused, unhappy, and frustrated. When Rob unfolded the early experience of his first conscious erection, Joan was surprised. She had never heard of this incident.

"You never told me about that," Joan said, "how can you remember something that happened when you were three years old and why didn't you mention it even once during all these years?"

"I don't know how or why I remember it," Rob replied, "I just know that from that moment on, stockings meant pleasure, love and good feelings to me. I kind of need them to have those feelings. Is that so wrong?"

Rather than answer the question Rob had posed as he faced me, I asked Joan, "When you and Rob were first married, making love frequently, feeling passionate and excited, were you at all turned off by his asking you to wear stockings, or his wearing or holding them. Did any of this bother you?"

"No, not really. It was exciting, different, and, besides, all of what we do is perfectly normal, oral sex and all that. The stockings don't interfere."

"Then perhaps you would like to answer Rob's question. Is that so wrong?"

Joan and Rob were very easy clients. It was gratifying to watch their instant and positive change. They saw me just twice, leaving after their second visit with smiles on their faces. During that session, they had recounted a night of, as they said, "Exquisite pleasure," in which they both wore stockings. Rob massaged Joan's legs and body for an hour, licking, kissing, and thanking her for understanding and loving him. Joan thanked him for loving her so much that he trusted her with his sexual fetish. She wanted to satisfy him in every way she could.

Sex therapy is quite often, quickly and completely successful. Often the client merely needs permission to do what they are doing. They need to feel "normal" and "OK." When the therapist says, yes, you are normal and OK, bells ring, champagne corks pop, and all is well with the world. Because guilt is often the culprit which controls the degree of pleasure you can experience, a professional "stamp of approval" is usually all that is needed.

In fact, a research project proved that most people need merely to know that they are normal, to feel better about themselves. A therapy clinic devised the following study:

1. *The first person to request therapy during the study, was given an appointment.*
2. *The second person to request therapy was told there was a four week waiting period, but their problem was not serious. They were assured they would be OK while they waited for an appointment.*
3. *The third person was told that they were OK and did not need therapy at all. It was recommended to them that they talk to a Priest, Rabbi, or friend if they wanted to, but that therapy was not necessary.*

The psychologists continued this with 130 patients. One third was given an appointment, one third waited four weeks, and one third was told therapy was not necessary.

Guess what? All 130 clients improved to the same degree, continued functioning, made positive choices in their lives, and felt fine about the decision made by the clinic. Those who waited for appointments, did not return; those who were told they did not need therapy, did not request it again; and those in therapy, made sufficient improvements to be terminated within a few months.

What is the dynamic here? Give a person a good feeling about themselves, tell them they are OK, and they will be OK. Remember, however, I am not discussing seriously disturbed, or physiologically impaired persons. The normal day to day neurotic like you and I responds very well to a pat on the back, a clear bill of health and the simple statement,

"You deserve to have pleasure in any way you want it as long as you are not hurting yourself or anyone else. Go for it! You are OK!" I think you will find that this dynamic holds true for most people in any, and all of life's circumstances!

REMEMBER:

Give yourself and your loved ones permission to GO FOR IT! You will be much happier, believe me! Rob and Joan are, and they are truly OK!

STAN AND CYNTHIA

One of the most unusual couples I met was Stan and Cynthia. I saw them only once, because all they needed was permission to continue to play-act their favorite "game."

Stan, a 42-year-old, Jay Leno look-a-like, had no idea where his "fetish" came from, or why he enjoyed it. He told me, "I would never tell anyone this; Cynthia and I really feel it should be a complete secret because it is so strange. It is not because I am ashamed or anything, just that it is our private 'thing.' Anyhow - I really enjoy imagining that Cynthia is giving birth to an egg. We put an egg into her vagina, and she kind of clucks and wiggles around as though she is in labor. I strut around crowing and flapping my arms like wings. When the egg drops out of Cynthia, I get so excited I often climax right then, without any other stimulation — no touching or anything. If not, we make love. Even if I do cum, we often make love and it's great."

70

It is during times like these that I truly appreciate "The Fuck-o-rama" class. I showed no shock or judgement at all. I sat quite relaxed and "poker-faced."

Cynthia, a sweet looking, "Annette Funicello" said, "I really like it, or I should say maybe I don't mind it. It is kind of fun watching Stan's excitement. He really goes wild, and we both benefit from it. As I move around, my breasts heaving, and my pelvic thrusting, it is a turn-on for me, too. So we were wondering what you think as a professional. Is there something wrong with us?"

I asked them the standard question. "Are you sure you both feel comfortable with this?"

They both responded that they did. I asked Cynthia again, "Cynthia, how do you feel about your part in this fantasy?"

She told me she enjoyed his pleasure, and also liked the feel of the egg inside of her and the feelings as she "gave birth to it."

"I love the control I have as I use my vaginal muscles to expel the egg," she related. "I feel kind of powerful, being able to do that."

I told them my philosophy and personal belief: "Anything that 'works' is perfectly normal, wonderful and acceptable as long as you are not hurting yourself, or anyone else." We hugged as we said goodbye and I wished them good luck and continued sexual pleasure.

It was only after they left that I realized I had not asked a crucial question. I am still curious as to whether the egg was raw, hard-boiled, peeled, cold, hot? I will never know because I felt it inappropriate to call and ask. I knew that as a therapist, I had no right to ask. After all, it doesn't seem relevant — does it?

71

HELEN AND DICK

There are many other clients with unusual sexual pleasures. Helen and Dick who play "Mommy and Daddy" with Daddy threatening Mommy if she doesn't behave he'll have to "have his way with her." Mommy teases Daddy "that he isn't a good daddy and can't have any goodies." They, too, merely needed permission to continue the game they found exciting and passionate. They visited me only once.

SANDY AND RANDALL

Sandy and Randall play "pick up" at least twice a month. He sits at a bar or restaurant. She picks him up. Often she wears wigs, unusual clothing. He wears disguises such as mustaches or beards, and hats. They turn each other on, teasing and taunting, playing at "pick up."

"When we do go home," Randall told me, "it's all hell breaking loose. Being out together, playing at courting and tempting each other again is just so romantic and wild; we love it."

Many couples have come to my office asking permission to use turn-on magazines, films, books, and even the Internet. Whatever works, whatever is good for both, whatever is a turn-on for passion and pleasure without hurting anyone - that's OK with me. I give couples permission to have pleasure and excitement. I tell them to GO FOR IT, and JUST DO IT, if it is fun for them, excitement for them, and pleasure for them.

LENNY AND SANDRA

Again, I have to stress, it's OK only if it doesn't hurt anyone. One couple, Lenny and Sandra, came to see me because they had been playing "Daddy and Baby" for 18 years and found it exciting. Sandra admitted she always was in love with her father, and pretending Lenny was her daddy was very exciting for her.

Sandra went to a therapist because she was having trouble with their 17-year-old son. The therapist told her their "game" was dangerous. She was warned to stop it immediately. When Lenny came to see me, he was desperate. Sandra had totally turned off; after 18 years of really good sex, she was no longer interested. The therapist had, unfortunately, given Sandra a guilt complex. She felt what she had been doing was destructive, even "crazy."

I gave them permission to continue. I said, "It is true some fantasy play could become destructive and out of hand. But, after 18 years of playing their own "game," it was certainly not probable anything negative would result from it. "Ignore the therapist's warnings," I added. "He obviously did not have the entire picture of your relationship and your sexual needs. Relax and enjoy as you have been doing all of these years. Go for it!" They thanked me, and left holding hands, sighing deep sighs of relief.

REMEMBER:

Every therapist has their own background and their own "agenda." Often this agenda is not in synch with yours. Do not feel that we, therapists, are perfect and infallible. Our own problems do sometimes inflict themselves inappropriately and even destructively. YOU know what's best for you - be sure to trust your instincts and believe in yourself. If it feels right, go with it. If it doesn't, look again. Trust your own feelings when choosing a therapist as well. If you are not comfortable, look elsewhere. We need to trust ourselves and our inner voice. It is usually right.

BEVERLY

Beverly was worried that if she continued to masturbate, she would never have pleasure with a man. I told her that masturbation was perfectly normal, and that when she did meet someone, her sexuality would be satisfied with him as well as it had been with the vibrator. I also told her that she may want to continue using the vibrator, as many couples do.

HAROLD

Harold felt threatened and inadequate because his wife wanted to use a vibrator. I told him, as I'd told Beverly, "Many couples use a vibrator as a part of their lovemaking. It is normal, healthy, and a very satisfying turn-on. I explained women often have different orgasms with masturbation than they do through sexual intercourse or oral sex. It was not a threat, or because he was inadequate; it was merely different." Harold accepted this. The vibrator became a part of their lovemaking without any negative or embarrassed feelings for either of them from that point on.

JUDY AND IVAN

Judy and Ivan wanted to learn how to enjoy sex. Ivan was insisting that without anal sex, he could never be really satisfied. After a few sessions, it was painfully obvious that Ivan was homosexual and wanted Judy in his life so that he could deny his true sexual identity. They separated, Ivan 'came out' and both of them found other partners. Because of instances such as this one, sex therapists do not always give permission or help a couple to accomplish what they say they want. As soon as I met Ivan, and heard the "need" in his voice, I was suspicious. He discussed his homosexuality with me on the second session which I asked him to come to alone. He was able to tell Judy about it during our third session. They are still friends, and thankful that they both discovered the truth.

Judy admitted, "I never even suspected that Ivan was gay. I love him so much, but I did not want to have anal sex. I came to you only to have a safe place to tell him that I was not interested in that, and was really afraid of it.

REMEMBER:
Not all men who like anal sex are gay. Please do not jump to that conclusion. However, if you are not interested, or do not feel comfortable with a form of sexual activity, be sure to stay in your own "comfort zone." Do not give in to someone else's needs, at the expense of your own. Do what pleasures YOU as long as it does not hurt anyone else, or YOURSELF.

INGRID

When someone is being hurt, I not only try to stop it, I often have to intercede. Ingrid, a 34-year-old divorced attorney came to see me on a Thursday afternoon. By Friday morning, I had taken steps to remove her four year old son from her home. This is why:

Ingrid presented a perfectly normal, sophisticated picture. She was intelligent, lovely to look at, and completely self-assured, or so it seemed.

"My lover and I have been living together for almost a year," she told me. "Lately, he has insisted that he involve Darren, my four year old son, in our sex life. He puts Darren on his back, telling him that he's taking a horsie ride. Darren holds on to him, while we have intercourse. I would like you to help me learn how to explain to Darren that what we are doing is fun, so that he does not have any bad impressions or fears because of it. I just want to make sure it is alright."

At this point, I was no longer a therapist, but a child rights advocate. I did not hold back my opinion, or allow Ingrid her feelings without my judgement or action. I told Ingrid as calmly as I could, since I was so outraged at what she had told me, "I am mandated to protect the innocent and to reveal behavior like this, since it is destructive to a child. There is no way for Darren to think that this is "fun." It is outrageous and shocking that a woman of your intelligence would even imagine that it is OK. My only hope is that you have come here knowing exactly what I would do, because you wanted me to do it. Hopefully, for whatever reason, because you could not say no to your lover, in order to protect your child, you came to me to do it for you."

I called child protective services and the child was removed from Ingrid's home. Ingrid's mother, Darren's grandmother, was given custody of Darren. Unbelievable as it may sound, Ingrid remained with her lover for another year. Although she filed for return of custody when her lover left her, it was not granted.

Ingrid returned to her mother's house to live, so she could be close to Darren. This seems to have worked very well. Darren is protected from his mother's poor judgement, but has her close to him. Ingrid's mother is also a kind and wonderful grandma to Darren. I do not know how Darren has developed since then. I lost contact with them when Darren was seven. At that time, he seemed well adjusted and without any emotional scars. I hope this remained so for the rest of his life.

CHAPTER THREE

The Failures
And The
Tragedies

I AM FOREVER THANKFUL that the very large majority of men and women who wanted my help were indeed helped. They left their therapy feeling more successful, more joyful, and more in control of their lives. However, as in any career, I experienced failures. Each of them is sadly painful to me, and remains in my memory as a tragedy. I feel the failure was ours, mine and theirs. They chose, yes chose, to remain buried in their pain and illness, refusing to work at changing their behavior and their lives. My techniques and skills did not reach them; their own barriers and denials were too strong, too determined, and too directed towards failure for them to be reached at all.

These men and women continued to believe and to perpetuate their belief that their misery was inevitable, unavoidable, and permanent. As my client, Krisy once said to me "It's the way it is." They rationalize that they can not do anything, that they have no power. This defense mechanism keeps them enslaved by their destructive beliefs. In actuality, they have a greater fear of becoming a person who deserves power, than of maintaining the status quo of helplessness. They are comfortable in their pain — they are used to it, and they maintain it.

Are you suffering emotional pain, which you are holding on to? Are you a "professional victim," refusing to help yourself, enjoying the secondary gains of your suffering? I hope you do not identify with any of my failures and tragedies. If you do, please seek help. Change is not only possible, it is necessary.

REMEMBER:

Pain is unacceptable for the normal person. We can all be normal if we work at it. It is only those who "give up" and refuse to change, who continue in their emotional agony. If there is a psychosis, or physiological reason for your distress, modern medicine is miraculous. There are medications and chemical treatments for even the most serious of emotional problems.

Do not avoid your problems or revel in the reasons for your unhappiness; just do something about it. Your childhood is over; your helplessness is over. YOU, as an adult, have control and power. Take it. YOU deserve a better life.

KRISY

When Krisy came to me, she asked, "Can you really get over your childhood if your father sexually abused you — is it really possible? I'm 46 years old, and I am still not over it."

I allowed her to continue, searching her face for an expression, some hint of what she was feeling. She appeared emotionally sterile, cold and numb, her dark eyes blank. The insipid smile she tried to force was almost grotesque, a mask of denial and unrealistic indifference.

"My father came in to my room whenever my Mom was out," she continued. "He would touch my back, his hands under my pajamas or shirt and would kiss my neck, and fondle my legs. He would touch me all over, never really trying to have intercourse with me, just putting his fingers into me, playing with my nipples, and sometimes kissing my vagina. I would sit paralyzed, unable to move or to speak as he told me how much he loved me. He'd say, 'this is because Daddy loves you, and wants to show you his love.'"

"When my mom was around, he would touch me a lot, stroking my back or arms, and my mom would scream at him, 'leave her alone you bastard.' I think she knew he did more when she was away. I don't really know. I never said anything – I just didn't talk. I was real shy and quiet, afraid of everything and angry all of the time. I did not have many friends because I was so withdrawn. Tell me the truth," she said to me, "what can you do for me that will help?" Before I could respond, she added, "I doubt if you can do anything,

I don't even know why I'm here, it's over and that is it. There is nothing I can do."

"What would you like to do?" I asked. When she did not reply, I repeated the question, adding, "What would you like me to do?"

"I want you to take it all away, and I do not know what I would like to do. I guess I would like to get married and have a normal life, one that is not so ugly and painful. All of the men in my life are totally wrong. I know that, but I can't help myself. They are great in bed, and that is what I want. I want to know that I am normal sexually, and if I have sexual pleasure with someone, it makes me feel better. That's what I want — to feel better."

"How are these men wrong?" I asked.

"Well, maybe they are not so wrong, but everyone tells me they are bad. One is married, has three children, and, I have to admit, is really ugly." As she smiled for the first time and seemed to be truly laughing and happy, my antennae went up as a warning signal flashed. Not only did she know he was ugly and wrong for her, she liked that he was. I listened carefully as she told her story.

TJ, as he was known, was cross-eyed, a different race, married, and the father of three children. He was a drug addict and didn't really seem interested in her at all. Krisy had her brother call TJ, asking him to meet her in a hotel room somewhere. Sometimes he would meet her. Most of the time, he didn't even show up. Her brother had to call in case TJ's wife or children, answered the phone. When TJ was arrested for sexually harassing a 15 year old girl, his arrest put an end to her obsession with him. Although Krisy was still interested, dreamt about and 'longed' for him, the impossibility of the situation, forced her to look elsewhere.

She had to move on. Because all of the men in her life were also married, another red flag went up for me – she did not feel she deserved a man of her own. All of them are abusive to her. She chased them, begged them to see her, and cried to them of her need for them.

Krisy told me that she was even involved with a motorcycle "freak," as she said. Not only was he so dirty that his dungarees could free stand on the floor, they were so soaked with oil and filth, the weight kept them upright. He was also a drunk and threw beer cans all over her apartment, not to mention he also abused her, physically, emotionally, and financially. She paid all of his expenses, as well as giving him "spending money."

"I would buy him gifts hoping he would come over to get them; I even followed him to his 'biker den' in a dangerous neighborhood, to try to get him to be with me just one more time."

As she told me this, Krisy become more and more animated. The numb and emotionless face disappeared and the more she told me of the abusive relationships she had been in, the more excited she became.

"How do you feel right now, as you speak of these experiences?" I asked her, wondering if she was aware of her own emotional transformation from dispassionate and disconnected, to involved and excited.

"What are you talking about? I bet you think I like this, you think I enjoy remembering all these humiliations. You think I am disgusting don't you! You think I should be shot or something!"

Krisy, like most clients, said what she was feeling in couched and safe terminology. Sometimes clients negate their real feelings. For example, if I ask how they are feeling, they may say, "Well, I'm not angry if that is what you mean." This response tells me immediately that they are angry. In Krisy's case, her words meant: "Yes, I am enjoying remembering these humiliations, and I am disgusting."

When she left our first meeting, I told her, "Please think about the way you've chosen to take care of yourself. Your behavior is doing something for you. I would like you to think about what it is doing."

I wanted Krisy to become conscious of the secondary emotional gains she was seeking. Each filthy man in her life, was the filthy father she despised. Each experience confirmed for her, she, too, was filthy and disgusting.

The destructive cycle is ugly and painful. It goes like this:

If my father treated me horribly, I must have been horrible – I must have deserved what he did to me. Therefore, if he is horrible, I am, too. And, because I enjoyed his touching sometimes, and did not stop him, I deserve to be punished.

Most clients in this cycle come to the following conclusion:

If I can relive these experiences and fight, and not be responsible for them or enjoy them, and take care of myself, maybe then I can deserve to change.

Reliving the cycle, Krisy found filthy men, one worse than the other. In her unconscious, she hoped to reject them, fight against them, and begin to believe she deserved better. Unfortunately, each experience fulfilled her psychological need to confirm that she deserved degradation and victimization. She needed to feel that she enjoyed it to continue the self-degradation and self-hatred. If she did reject these behaviors, she would be on the road to health, which is not what she was able to accept, nor what she wanted.

Without some strength in herself to hold on to, she failed time and again, to win even one emotional battle. What she was getting out of these choices, was familiarity. Too often, our comfort zone is what we know, however horrible it is. We are so afraid of change, we hold on to what we have. Krisy held on very tightly.

Throughout our next sessions, I tried finding a glimmer of light, a ray of hope. We worked on her intellectual ability, attempting to make this the cornerstone upon which she could develop some emotional power. Krisy never really believed she was intelligent, which she admitted when she told me, "I'm just lucky. My job is easy, I do it well, and I keep getting promoted. Anyone can do it like I do, I was in the right place at the right time."

We also tried to work on her attractiveness. Krisy believed that she was very unattractive. Although she was beautiful, she was also overweight; the extra pounds hid her dramatic and striking features. Krisy often asked, "Why should I try to lose weight? Thin or fat, I never look good."

Krisy used the therapy sessions to confirm all that she wanted to believe about herself. She often said, "You don't even like me, you don't even think I'm normal, you probably are disgusted with me." Although I never manifested any judgementalism towards her, and although Krisy would hug and kiss me at the end of each session, she continued to insist that I didn't like her and she didn't like me. She did this to keep herself the unwanted, unloved, abused victim.

I recommended that Krisy see a psychiatrist who could write a prescription, which might alleviate some of her feelings of depression, as well as her insomnia. I told her I would continue to see her, and that our sessions might be more productive with the additional help she would receive from the medication. She refused, using this as proof that I wanted to "get rid of her."

My sadness was apparent on our last session, when I asked Krisy to take the time to develop a plan of attack.

"Write out a daily plan," I told her. "Who will you see, who will you not see? Write a short sentence next to each name saying why you are keeping them in your life and why you are not – be sure to include Satin (a new man in her life who was married, a gambler, and an alcoholic)."

"Also be sure to include your brother," I added. He was a viciously cruel man who was an unemployed thief and liar, and who took as much of Krisy's money as he possibly could. Sadly, he manifested the same pedophiliac abusive behavior towards his daughters that their father perpetrated on Krisy.) "Be sure to also include John," I continued. He was a man Krisy worked with who was trying to become closer to her, and who was actually a decent human being.

Finally, I recommended that she keep a log of what she did, and what she wanted to do, as well as how she felt about different choices."

I wanted Krisy to become more conscious of her day to day experiences. I hoped she would see, by writing down her behaviors and choices, how self-destructive she was. I thought that if she wrote her own words, begging Satin to see her, or if she saw the cold fact of how much money she gave her brother each week, she would see the moment just prior to those acts, during which she had a choice. She could hang up the phone when calling Satin and she could throw her brother out of her home, and refuse to give him another dime. She could also refuse Paul, the married man who visited her at 3:00 a.m., and who left her by 3:20 after sex.

"Call me every afternoon, and we'll talk about your log, if you need to," I told her. "Bring it to your next session so that we can work with it. I want you to have a lot of good and positive experiences under your belt. I want you to see where your power is, and how much of it you have. If you take the moment to write what you are planning to do, you will see it more clearly, and perhaps you will make wiser choices."

Krisy called a few times. She continued to see Satin, as often as he would see her, and to give her brother money; she actually gave him two credit cards for which she was responsible. She also continued to hate herself and to punish herself accordingly. All of the assertiveness training we'd done together, and all of the ego building, the meditation techniques, the visualization, the building of awareness of what she was doing to herself, and the fact that she did not have to continue doing these things was wasted.

I was ineffective. It is also true that Krisy chose to fail. I do not know if someone else would have been able to help her. My recommendations that she see another therapist were completely ignored and refused. Krisy ended up calling to cancel her sessions, and to tell me that she would not be seeing me again. She had not kept the log because, as she said, "I don't want to see what I do, it's ridiculous."

Krisy called me a year after our last session; she was suffering from AIDS. She wasn't even sure which of her partners had infected her. There were so many possibilities. Despite the scourge of this deadly disease, Krisy continued having unsafe sex with a multitude of unsafe partners.

Sadly, Krisy died three years later. I went to her funeral and met her brother for the first time. He was obese, sloppy and truly grotesque looking. He was actually laughing as he said, "Well I guess you're not so great, are you, she's dead anyhow." His inference that I could have saved her did not go undetected. I know I could not have saved her, she had to want to save herself. Instead, she chose to remain a victim, to prove to the world that her father had destroyed her, when in fact, she had destroyed herself. Her father began the process, yes, but she continued it, and sadly, she also finished it.

SHARON

Sharon was a strikingly beautiful woman. She looked like Jackie Kennedy in style, face and figure. She had real class — pzzzazzz. I was totally amazed to discover that beneath this absolutely perfect facade was a hopeless self-destructive woman.

Sharon was raised in a junkyard — literally. Her father's junkyard business surrounded their home. She had to walk through, as she said,

"Mountains of filthy, smelly junk, before I could get to the street." When she described her childhood to me, she said, "We lived, ate, slept, and smelled junk all of the time. My dad brought things into the house, which he said were the 'good things.' They were as horrible as everything else. The house always smelled moldy and old. My mattress had holes in it, and although I could hardly sleep because I was covered by bug bites, my father would not change the mattress. After I saw bedbugs on the sheet, when I was five years old, I began sleeping on the floor. My mom never changed her dress — at least I don't think she did. My sister left home when she was 14. I left three years later, when I was 15."

She summed it all up by saying, "I've made a wonderful life for myself; I have a great job as a stockbroker, I have money, my apartment is immaculate and so am I. You can see that can't you?" she finally asked as she looked at me imploringly, her face becoming anxious and sad. She looked about five years old.

"What do I see, Sharon? You tell me?"

"OK, play the psyche game. Don't tell me anything," she responded. "I'll play, too. You see a gorgeous woman; I know how I look. I am pretty and I dress great and have even been offered modeling jobs several times," she added as her face changed again. She was once again composed and self-assured – an assertive, confident adult. "What you don't know is what is inside of me. I'm one big junkyard. I am filthy and smelly, and I hate myself for it. I can't empty myself out. I vomit everyday, and I bathe three, even four times a day. Nothing changes how I feel about myself. The worst part is that I'm frightened of my behavior. I am doing very self-destructive things, punishing myself — hoping to cleanse myself somehow, and I know I need help before it gets worse."

"Do you want to talk about the 'things' you are doing?"

She replied with a sigh of relief, slumped into her chair and said very quietly, "I pick up men, any men – the cheaper, the more slovenly and the more dangerous the better. I go to small neighborhood bars, out of the way bars, dirty cheap bars, and I find men there. I even bring them home with me. You want to hear something really crazy? I had the best sex of my life with a guy who had crabs. I actually felt myself climax each time a crab would jump in his pubic hair. I lay there staring, watching for them to jump. Nuts, right?"

I said nothing.

"Can I stop doing this? Can you make me stop doing this?"

We worked for five weeks. Sharon had extremely emotional moments while recreating and reliving some of her childhood: screaming at her mother for allowing her to live in such filth, begging her sister not to leave her alone, never having a friend, being humiliated and made fun of in school, the bulimia she developed to keep herself clean — all of it. Sharon not only talked, but had emotional catharsis, crying, vomiting, screaming in pain during the sessions. She truly seemed to be able to 'get it all out' and 'cleanse herself.'

Fritz Perls, a noted psychologist and founder of Gestalt Therapy, told me during my training with him, "Don't carry your burdens on your back. Examine them, accept them, and then swallow them. They will disperse within you and will not be as heavy or painfully destructive as they were on your back."

Although Sharon was able to do this, the agony remained with her. She continued to date and sleep with "her father."

Men as drunk, as filthy and as unkind as he was, were the only men she seemed able to relate to or enjoy.

It seems psychologically true that a young woman feels a great deal of guilt when her life seems to be "better" than her mother's life. It is difficult to accept that your mother, the woman who nurtured and loved you, cared for and protected you, lived a life of misery. Sharon's guilt and shame kept her from overcoming her past, from surpassing her mother. Instead, she recreated her mother's life in the way that was most horrible to her — sex with "animals like her father."

Sharon had an appointment with me on a Tuesday in June, just after Memorial Day Weekend. When she didn't show, I called her apartment. I then called her doorman. He told me Sharon had been found murdered in her living room. She died sometime Friday or Saturday, but had not been found until Tuesday morning by the housekeeper.

The powerful tentacles of our childhood have the ability to dig deeply into our psyche and hold fast. Unless we can rip them out one by one, and accept the pain of our own bleeding wounds, we allow ourselves to perpetuate the rhythm of that childhood. Unless we can see the joy and the grace of the power of choice, the power of positive, constructive change and the beauty of our own futures, we cannot tear away the destructive holds our childhoods created. Sharon failed. I failed. Her parents failed.

Her tragedy is a lesson for all parents. Realize that what you do to your children, with your children, and for your children, stays with them all of their lives. Clients have told me hundreds of times about one remark, or one behavior, which caused lifetime scars.

Jan always remembered her mom asking, *"Why can't you be as pretty as your sister?"*

Phil hears his dad's voice every day of his life saying, *"You'll always be a fat and worthless pig."*

Don knows now what his mom said came from her own illness and emotional void, but he can still hear her telling him, *"I was in labor four days with you, and this is how you act? A bum, a dirty bum, that's all you are."*

Helen has been able to confront and extract an apology from her mother for the constant remarks, *"Helen, you are a clumsy ass, you'll never get through life the way you are."* Helen had six broken bones before she was nine years old. Her mother's predictions were very much a part of Helen's clumsiness. She was the classic example of the "self-fulfilling prophesy." Often, we need the love and attention of our parents so much that we actually do what they say we'll do, however ridiculous or destructive it is.

What you hear, is what you become. What you see, is what you become. Your parents act as role models for you; their behavior teaches you more than anything else in your childhood. Love, affection, respect and kindness create joyous children and successful happy adults; opposite emotions teach opposite lessons.

REMEMBER:

You can and do overcome your childhood nightmares. It is so much better if you don't have any. Many children remain in their pain, adulthood does not take it away without effort, great effort. If you keep trying, you can succeed. Do not let your childhood nightmares control you. YOU, as an adult, have choices! Take control now!

DEBBIE

Debbie was a 22 year old journalism student well on her way to not only her Masters Degree in journalism, but a great career with a major magazine. While researching the S & M phenomenon for her Masters thesis, she attended various meetings and clubs, interviewed sadists and masochists, bondage experts, dominatrixes, masters and slaves. At one of the meetings, she was confronted by "Rock" a 6'3" extremely handsome amateur wrestler. He seemed wonderful to Debbie, who told me, "I thought that we would have the most beautiful children the instant I met him. We are both so blonde, and have really big blue eyes, and his features are as nice as mine." She knew she was beautiful and was able to say this without any vanity or conceit. It was a matter of fact.

She continued, "I seemed so drawn to him, thinking about having kids with him and all, I just didn't even wonder what he was doing there and what it would mean to my future."

They had several dinners together, and she told him she was writing her thesis. He gave her a great deal of information about the S & M scene, and about himself as a wrestler, writer, and lover. At no time did she think of asking him what his sexual propensities were. She trusted and liked him, or as she said, "I fell into him like milk poured into a glass. I felt so safe and smooth; it felt like love to me. We had fun together, we laughed and talked, and we had wonderful sex. There was no hint that he was involved in the scene."

After three weeks, Debbie's parents met Rock, liked him, and made plans to invite him to their weekend home in The Hamptons, on Long Island. Debbie was not seen again for five months after the lovely dinner the four of them shared.

A desperate call from Debbie finally came. When her mother went to meet her, Debbie was almost incoherent.

"Debbie was filthy dirty," her mother told me. "I couldn't believe a girl who was so immaculate could look like that. She hadn't bathed in weeks, maybe more. She was bruised on most of her body, her eyes glazed, her body emaciated. I couldn't stop crying as we drove home from the coffee shop where I picked her up."

Debbie's own story emerged a few days later in my office. She sat between her mother and father, both of them obviously loving and protective parents. They held her hands and stroked her as she spoke. "It started like fun. Rock asked if he could tie me to the headboard before we made love. I was kind of scared but excited. I can't tell you how passionate it was." Before going on, she looked at her mother and said, "I don't want to hurt you mom, but I have to tell the truth. The sex was like nothing I *ever* imagined. When I wanted to get up, Rock playfully put a large leather collar around my neck, attached a leash to it, and led me into the bathroom. When I came out, he asked if I would crawl on my hands and knees just to have fun. He said, 'Make believe I'm your trainer and you are a baby bear.' He said he wanted to take care of the 'ittie bittie baby bear.' I kind of laughed and again we had great sex right there on the floor."

Debbie's Dad was very flustered and uncomfortable. He asked if it was advisable that he remain in the room. Debbie said it would be better if he left, that she would be more comfortable. I realized how sensitive and empathic this young woman was. Despite her own tears and difficulty in remembering her captivity, she found a place to recognize her Dad's needs and to respond. He left very relieved, kissing and telling her, "I love you very much, it is just hard for me to hear about this. Whatever happened, I love and respect you, remember that."

Debbie even walked him to the door, hugged and kissed him and said that she understood, and felt better herself not having to humiliate herself in front of him.

When we continued talking, she said the sex was always fabulous. Debbie described multiple orgasms that seemed to vibrate within her entire body for hours. The humiliation and control increased proportionally to the sexual pleasures. It seemed the more control and abuse Rock foisted upon her, the more sexual pleasure she would anticipate. Her expectations would be fulfilled.

"It was as though I was in a trance. I felt nothing but the excitement and anticipation of what I was going to feel. I did not think at all; I was almost like a vegetable responding to water, sunlight and food. I would flower and grow when his body came to mine, feeling nothing during the torture that preceded it. At first, I tried to leave. I had to go to school, see friends, my parents, everything. But Rock wouldn't let me leave. I was terrified, but so satisfied sexually, that whatever I said, or tried to do, he would ignore. I was truly a captive, but I liked it. Did you ever hear of the Stockholm Syndrome? Well I had it a million percent."

"After about three months of the bad always being followed by the ecstasy, she continued, "it became only bad. Rock told me that I wasn't really able to help him to become the 'best master' he could possibly be. He explained that the 'best master' had a very compliant slave, one who would suffer anything, comply with everything. He demanded that I begin to accept more and more, without being rewarded for my 'good behavior.' If I would refuse the rewards, then I would really prove myself. He wanted me to refuse to have sex with him, to tell him that I didn't need anything from him, other than to be controlled by him. I had to prove myself or he would not 'succeed.' I tried, hard as it is to believe. I tried to do everything he wanted. I even tried to refuse to have sex with him, but I couldn't."

At this point, Debbie turned to her mother and asked her, "Mom, please go outside with Dad, I don't want you to hear anymore of this. It's all the same and I know it's as hard for you as it is for him."

Not accepting her mom's protests, she insisted that her mom leave. Debbie walked her to the door, hugged her and told her that she loved her. Again, I was impressed with Debbie's warmth and understanding.

"I just can't say these things in front of her, not anyone really. But I know that if I don't get them out, the memories will fester inside of me, poisoning me forever."

Debbie was absolutely correct. Unspoken painful memories do fester and continue to poison your psyche as well as your soul. It is a truism that the depth and degree of the secrets you keep are directly commensurate with the level of your psychological illness. Secret keeping is motivated by shame, a corrosive element which eats away at you, destroying your life, rendering you impotent, and completely controlled by your "secrets."

As Debbie exposed her shame and humiliation to the light of day, she also exposed it to herself and to me. My reaction was crucial. I was Debbie's conscious, her judge and jury. As she spoke, I maintained eye contact and had no expression at all other than intent concentration and interest.

"I would beg him to have sex with me," she continued. "I told him that I'd do anything if only it could be the way it was. He kept escalating what I had to do, saying that if I succeeded, he would reward me. Then it would be something else. He kept me tied to the dining room table for two days, promising that if I didn't eat or drink, or ask for anything until he offered, he would fuck me. I could go to the bathroom, but nothing else."

"I did what he wanted," Debbie admitted, "but he still broke his promise. But, you know what, the worst part is that I was beginning to feel strong, really powerful, like I was the one in control. I felt that I was able to accomplish the task put before me, and that by doing my 'job' so to speak, I was the winner, the hero. It's crazy, I know, but the more I did what he wanted, the stronger I felt."

97

"Then he began to cut me," she went on. "Before that, there were some punches and choking, black and blue marks from pulling and pushing, but nothing as serious as the razor blade. The first time he cut me, he kept kissing me while he did it. Then he made love to me, smearing the blood all over our bodies. I was absolutely wild with him, so grateful for his body, his love, I didn't care what he did to me."

"Of course it escalated," Debbie continued. "I knew that it would, and I wanted it to. I felt I would be a better person if I could put up with everything, anything. Besides, I was getting sex again, sex I felt I would die without. I had to get it no matter how."

Rock had convinced Debbie that the more pain she could bear, the stronger she was, the more humiliation she took, the more she developed her character and the more control she allowed Rock, the more control she really had herself. This is typical thinking in the S & M world. The slave has the control. The master follows her lead. The more the slave cues the master to do, the stronger they both are.

Debbie hung her head and began to cry as I sat quietly, not wanting to interrupt her. I watched this beautiful young woman sob hysterically as she curled up like a fetus, flailing her arms at the air, crying out, "God help me, God help me."

After a long time, during which she scratched herself, tore at her hair, sobbed, drooled, and cried, I asked very quietly, "Help you how Debbie? How can God help you?"

She looked up at me, her eyes wide with fright, as close to terror as I'd ever seen in anyone and said, "Help me to stop wanting him, help me to live without him. I know that if I had stayed he would have killed me. I knew before I finally left that I had to get away from him, or maybe I'd even kill myself by following all of his dictates. Finally, it was too much. When he went to work, I just walked out and called my mom. But God help me, I still want him, I still want him."

Rock had cut Debbie in about 50 different places. He made small, shallow cuts which were not life threatening before urinating over Debbie — the urine burning her torn flesh. He would then put a clock in front of Debbie's face and tell her to lie there for one full hour.

"You can take a shower after an hour," he would say. "Remember, if you want to be in control, lie there for an hour. Take the pain. Take whatever I give you. If you can be the best slave by obeying me, I can be the best master. I need you, sweetheart. I need you to be good, so we can win together, so we can both be the best. This is the final test Debbie. This is it — then we can fuck for a few days. You will love it, I promise." Debbie looked up to see my blank expression. "Have you heard anything like this before?" she asked.

The time was right for me to show my acceptance of her, to help her to accept herself. I took Debbie in my arms and held her saying, "Yes, I have heard these horrors before, but your suffering is not to be compared to others. You have suffered intolerably, and you have overcome the agony. I am so proud of you, and so grateful that you have come out of this pain. You are a hero, a truly strong hero who has taken total control of her life. From this moment on, your life will be whatever you want it to be. You are strong, and perfect. You are a hero to yourself and to everyone who loves you."

After a few moments she moved away from me and asked, "How can you be proud of me? I have been, and am, so disgusting; I feel worthless and I am worthless."

99

"You have lived through a horrible, degrading and seemingly self-destructive five months," I told her. "Yes, you took part in it. Yes, you enjoyed some of it. And, yes, you felt that you needed Rock no matter what you had to do to get him. Although all of this is true, the most important factor here is that Rock is in jail facing abuse and kidnapping charges. You are sitting here working to overcome the horror of these months. You have taken control! You have realized how dangerous Rock is and you are testifying against him so that he can not hurt anyone else! You are here to accept the past as a mistake, and to go on to a future which will prove your strength and your goodness! For all of these reasons, I am proud of you!"

Rock was sentenced to three years in jail while Debbie wrote her story, and received her Masters degree. Although she seemed to be fine, she did not date, or see her friends as regularly as she used to. She took a course with me in assertiveness training at a local university, and she continued to see me for several sessions. She gained weight, was physically healthy, and although she was desperately sad most of the time, she was working as a journalist, her life's dream. And apparently she did very well at her job; she received two raises in three months, and won a small award for one of her investigative reports.

When Rock was to be released from jail, I called Debbie, asking her to be careful. I knew that he had threatened to kill her for testifying against him, and deep down, I was fearful that he could still exercise sexual control over her. She assured me that she was fine, and that the district attorney had assured her that he would not dare even contact her.

Debbie's parents called me just three weeks later. Debbie had moved to San Francisco with Rock. They were, Debbie told them, "very happy and doing well. He's not into that stuff anymore. He was rehabilitated in jail, and he really loves me. Don't worry, we're fine."

Debbie was working at a newspaper while Rock was working as a male dancer in one of the local clubs. After a few months went by, Debbie visited her parents and she did truly seem fine. She looked good, and as her mother said, "I looked all over her body, and there wasn't a mark. I do feel much better now that I am sure."

Tragically, Debbie was eventually found at the emergency room entrance of a hospital in Oakland, California, just outside of San Francisco; someone had left her there. She died a few hours later. She was dehydrated, and infected with raging bacteria in multiple unattended wounds covering 70% of her body. Rock was nowhere to be found.

Her mothers words, "I feel much better," were echoed by most of Debbie's friends, relatives, and co-workers. Everyone who knew her reflected on her sadness, but also remarked about her productivity, her involvement with her job, and her warm and kind behavior towards everyone. We all, myself included, felt her sadness was natural; she had lived a nightmare, and survived. Debbie couldn't be expected to heal completely and run around joyously after her ordeal. No one expected that she would ever return to that horror.

Debbie's words continue to echo in my mind "God help me, I still want him, I still want him." Unfortunately, when she opened her life to him, she allowed her prophesy to come true; he did kill her.

What was in Debbie's background which could have allowed her behavior to reach the level of self-destructiveness it did? What could have been done to save her? Who could have intervened? Where was God to help her? Where was I to help her? Will Rock ever be punished for his crime? There are no answers, only more questions.

REMEMBER:

Perhaps the most important question of all is one you can answer: What are you doing to love yourself, care for yourself, and be good to yourself? What do you deserve from this life and how are you getting it? This is your question. Hopefully, you have found, and will continue to find, all the right answers.

BEN

 Ben met me at the airport in Fort Lauderdale. He was, as advertised, an absolutely stunning clone of Frank Sinatra, and just as charming. Ben had called asking me to spend an entire weekend of intensive therapy with him. Although the money he offered was very tempting, and staying at a fine hotel on the beach sugared the request, I was genuinely intrigued with Ben's problem.

"I cannot get rid of my obsession with cleanliness," he told me after our first telephone conversation. "I know I'm nuts. Everyone around me knows I'm nuts, but I can't stop. If I touch anything, I wash my hands. If someone visits, I wash the chair they sat on. I run my dishwasher twice, sometimes three times, if anyone eats or drinks from my things. My clothes are all done twice in very hot water. I've gone through dozens of housekeepers; none of them are good enough. One actually quit because I wanted her to sterilize the iron every time she used it. I need help. Could you please come down here and clear out whatever cobwebs I must have to be so crazy?"

I cleared my calendar for a four day trip to Florida. My goal was to have Ben experience the "real world" — dirt, mess and all. If he survived the days I was there, perhaps he could overcome his obsessive-compulsive behavior. I intended to desensitize him constantly, creating dirt and mess, while he used relaxation techniques to help him bear the process.

Although the perks were, as I said, very tempting, the challenge was too great to deny. I love a fight, especially a difficult one. And, it was a fight. Ben agreed to my terms, accepting that he would be put through the wringer in order for me to treat him.

As we drove in his convertible, he again reiterated that he would "do whatever you say I should do, I promised, and I will."

I began immediately touching him while he drove. I touched his arms, his shoulders, the dashboard, the wheel. I said nonchalantly, "You know I haven't washed my hands since arriving, I must have newsprint on them from reading on the plane. I wish I had washed after lunch, airplane food is so messy. I am glad I had eight quarters for the tip I gave the redcap. I did not have any small bills." Remarks like these made Ben wince again and again. I had planned it this way. Each time he winced, I would say, "Take a deep breath. You can get through this. Concentrate on your breathing and say silently, 'It is OK, I can get through this.' "

After I checked into my hotel, I insisted on going straight to his place. In response to his asking if I wanted to freshen up a bit before we left, I said, "No, we have to begin work right now, we do not have much time."

I had a ball, but Ben did not let go. He did what I wanted him to, but his deep-seated need for perfection and control did not abate. After I pushed him out of his motor boat onto a muddy beach, he was forced to wear his filthy white shorts for several more hours because he had no change of clothing. Although he washed in the ocean it was not satisfactory to him. We ate lobster on the beach from a huge pail of lobster and shrimp. We melted butter over the same fire we had cooked the fish on, and rubbed the lobster and shrimp with butter before we ate it. We used fingers and lips, no utensils. Ben did all of this, and even smiled once in a while. Even though he actually enjoyed the picnic, he ran into the ocean a few times during our feast, to wash himself.

After I threw his comb away, his discomfort was obvious as he was used to combing his hair frequently. Because he also did not have a mirror to look at while we were boating, swimming or eating, he was also nervous. Throughout it all he kept saying, "This is really fun, I wish I could do these things all the time," even though he really did not want to; he was just giving lip service to the situation.

Each of these experiences was preceded by quiet meditation, and practicing the deep breathing and relaxation techniques. I had Ben imagine doing what we were going to do. At the same time his mind focused on future behaviors; he was to try to keep his body quiet, his breathing relaxed, his mind clear. When we were actually experiencing the food, the dirt, the rolling in the mud, I spoke quietly, to bring him through relaxation techniques, "Breathe deep. Bring the air in. Hold. Let the air out. Keep your breathing deep and quiet."

Although he saw that his physiology was responding to the relaxation, despite his behavior, and that he could indeed learn to control the anxiety and the internal pressures to 'cleanse himself,' he refused to continue. Although Ben had told me how his problems interfered with his life, he accepted them because they were comfortable and familiar; he needed the problems more than he needed to change. He was even able to describe the painful incidents in his life without manifesting any discomfort or emotional pain.

"When I make love to a woman, I keep several wash clothes around, to wash and wipe her in various parts of her body," he told me. I don't want to kiss a part that I haven't washed. Of course we take showers first, but sometimes, I even want to take a shower during our lovemaking. I will stop after kissing for a while, wanting to jump back into the shower."

Ben has also never performed cunnilingus, nor does he enjoy kissing with his mouth open. He kisses with, as he said, "My lips – that feels good, I don't need to use my tongue, or to have her put her tongue into my mouth. That is pretty dirty; there are all kinds of germs in the mouth."

After making love, Ben would change the sheets, and the woman would sleep in the guestroom. All of her clothing and other belongings would have to be kept in the guestroom, as he didn't like to mix anything with his things. Ben's habits were extraordinary. He would actually get out of the shower if he had to urinate. He would wipe himself dry, urinate, then get back into the shower. When I told him that most people would just urinate, and not think anything about it, he was mortified, asking in a very shocked and incredulous voice, "How could anyone do such a thing? It is a filthy thing to do!" I don't know about you, but everyone I've asked thinks that it is Ben who is weird, and not those of us who are more natural with our bodies.

Ben does not have a problem attracting women. His money, looks and charm can win the most attractive women. He's dated heiresses and actresses, some of whom I have met. I actually had the opportunity to work with two of his women. Both were hopeful that he could change. They were, as they said, "in love with him when he acted normally."

It is interesting that Ben has no recollection of being oppressed as a child, forced to be immaculate, punished if he dirtied himself, or harshly toilet trained.

"My mom was very beautiful, well groomed and perfectly behaved," he told me. She never restricted my activities. I could do what I wanted to, it just did not seem like fun to me to play ball and get all sweaty, or ride a bike, or anything like that. I enjoyed tennis, and golf, and still do; it is so civilized. I shower at the club, wear whites, look good, and feel clean. I like those things."

"Dad," he remarked, "was different. Because he was somewhat sloppy, Mom got on his case a great deal. I did not like to kiss him when he smelled sweaty and dirty after working in the garden, or riding his horse. He would try to pick me up, or put me on the horse, or hug me, and I would feel very skeeved out, like chalk on a blackboard or something; I just did not like it. But, it was no big deal. He would go take a shower and hug me. We were very close. I love both parents a lot. In fact, we still get together a few times a week. I enjoy their company and am lucky to have them."

Ben's attitude about his own behavior was deeply entrenched. He felt he was weird, and that his habits alienated him quite often. But, he was also convinced that his ways were the right ways. His childhood memory of disgust with his own father if he was not perfectly groomed, is still the bit in his mouth, pulling him away from anything that even faintly resembles what disgusted him as a child.

He could not imagine anyone not changing the sheets after making love, or being sure that their bodies were clean all the time during lovemaking. Memories of not wanting to kiss his father controlled his psyche, terrifying him that his partner may not want to kiss him if he was disheveled or rumpled from lovemaking. He did not understand how anyone could hang their clothes in a closet with someone else's clothes, or not wash linens and other things at least twice to be sure they were clean. After all, his father had probably put his gardening things into the closet with his mother's clothing, or even washed those clothes with other 'cleaner' things. His obsession stemmed from these childhood memories which were so offensive to him, he needed to avoid any repetition of such feelings in himself or in anyone else.

Ben was a delightful friend and companion. Our weekends in Florida were truly fun and a welcome respite from the winds and snow of New York's winter. I tried every behavior modification program and technique I knew. I taught Ben desensitization so that he could sleep with his sexual partners and not delegate them to the guestroom. He also learned to avoid the washcloth during sex, although the showers continued. On a scale of one to ten, Ben improved to a five or six. But because his habits were still so exaggerated, few people could tolerate his needs.

For example, Ben's highest level of accomplishment in his quest for a more normal life, was to take three showers a day and change his clothing each time, a goal most of us find unacceptable. He agreed that sterilizing the iron was ridiculous, but demanded the housekeeper change the ironing board cover each and every time there was any ironing done. Even if Ben reached his goal of ten, or his complete cure, he would be far below most of us, with still very unacceptable demands and behaviors.

Because Ben never dealt with the real root of his obsessiveness, I felt that I failed. I could not intellectually or otherwise reach Ben to pierce the balloon of unrealistic expectations of himself and others.

I worked with two women Ben thought he loved and who claimed they loved him. Both left him, unable to deal with his idiosyncrasies. One of the women, Harriet, asked me, "What would you do?" I answered honestly, "I would be unable to tolerate his demands and behavior."

"Then why are you working with him, and with me?" she asked. Again, I honestly said, "The human spirit is indomitable, there is always hope. I know he can love, I know he can show this love; it is just a matter of time and motivation. I also know, you do not want to wait that long, and more importantly, Ben does not seem to be motivated.

I am sorry. But, I keep trying because I see the glimmer of hope, and want him to see it, too."

Although Ben is rich, handsome, charming, physically healthy, and is as immaculately clean as his two homes and three automobiles, he is alone.

"You know," he told me, "life is a bit lonely sometimes, but it is better than constantly holding myself back from screaming because things are not the way I need them to be."

Upon hearing this, I felt my own failure, and of course regretted adding this failure to the others. I regret that I was not able to convince Ben to take the power from his "critical child" and assert his adult power over his obsessive, self-destructive behaviors. As he said, he felt he would rather not "scream when things are wrong" than live a more pleasured, connected life.

It always amazes me how strong our childhood influences are, and how weak we keep our adult controls. Ben's situation and failure certainly reiterate my amazement. But then, I know of hundreds — yes hundreds — of my own clients who took their "childhood Circe" by the neck, choked it until it had not a breath left, threw it away into the recesses of their minds, and allowed the adult to live his or her life, completely, to the fullest extent of joy and pleasure.

These are the clients who give me faith and trust in the power of our own psychological strengths. My experience gives me the knowledge that all of us, yes, all of us, can overcome what has happened in the past, keep it in the past, and forge forward to a bright and magical future.

One of my favorite sayings is, "Make Life Happen." I say it at the end of each of my radio shows. It epitomizes my philosophy that we should take positive action, rather than being reactive.

REMEMBER:

Be in control of your life. Don't let it just happen. Make it happen the way you want it to. You really do have that power. Make your life happen now!

CHAPTER FOUR

♂Attitudes &
♀Behaviors

OUR BEHAVIORS ARE BASED on our attitudes. If we feel entitled to good treatment from others, we will behave that way. A wonderful example of this is a friend of mine who was shopping in Tiffany's in New York. The saleswoman was extremely rude, especially for a shop like Tiffany's. My friend asked her one question, "Did your mother raise you to believe that you are as good as everyone else?"

The saleswoman replied very curtly, "Of course she did, how dare you ask me such a question."

My friend leaned close to the saleswoman and asked her in a very quiet and kind tone, "Then why don't you behave as though you believe it?"

People who feel good about themselves, who like themselves, and who truly trust themselves, express these feelings to others. They like people, they trust them, and they treat others well. They do not have to be rude, or nasty, or express any 'superior' attitudes. They are who they are, and they exude a sense of satisfaction.

The attitudes we have about human sexuality are deeply imbedded in our psyche, and are expressed on a daily basis. We dress in certain ways, which express our feelings about our bodies. We keep in shape, or not, according to how much we truly care about and respect our health and our bodies. We use the condition of "overweight" to fend off sexual feelings or sexual overtures of others, and we also use our looks and appearance as defense mechanisms against intimacy and passion. In some cases, we even portray the looks and behavior of sexually liberated and passionate people as a way of hiding our own inhibitions and sexual fears. For example, we may dress so that our bodies are not obvious, hidden under loose clothing. We may even gain weight to hide our sexuality, or we may go in the opposite direction — dressing seductively to hide our shyness.

Our appearance is also often confusing to others, in that we give one message about our attitudes, even though we truly feel quite the opposite. You and your lovers know the truth behind what you are expressing. The questions to ask are whether you want to continue to express one attitude and whether your attitudes and feelings are getting in the way of your pleasures, feelings of satisfaction and love. Can you change? Do you want to change? If so, what do you want to change? What is going on right now in your life that is an impediment to a more complete, more satisfactory relationship sexually and emotionally? Which of your childhood attitudes is controlling you? Which of the "no-no's" of your early years are still resounding in your mind? Which of them are still holding you by the throat like the tentacles of an octopus, pushing you in directions you really don't want to go?

In my practice, I meet many couples who have these tentacles wrapped around their lives, keeping them from intimacy and closeness. They know they want more, but aren't sure what to do with the controls their past has on them. I have developed a very simple questionnaire which helped them to break through their bondage, in a "here and now" way. Rather than go back into the past, and become involved in long-term therapy, I feel that the answers to these questions might open doors to new adventures and new permissions. I feel their thoughts, and their responses serve as break-throughs, which can be strong enough to overcome old belief systems. For many couples, the answers to these questions unlock a deeper understanding of their partner, enhanced sexual adventures, and a more secured love.

The following is the questionnaire:

1. I wish I could...

2. I wish you would...

3. To me oral sex is...

4. To me anal sex is...

5. What do you think of threesomes and using a vibrator?

6. My fantasy is...

7. What I really love is...

8. After we make love, please...

9. What will you NEVER do?

10. What do I do that you do not like?

I suggest that you and your partner answer these questions separately. Share the answers with each other and discuss your responses. When you have done this, and had a few hours to digest the results, then, and not until then, continue reading. The following are responses three couples had to these questions, and what happened to them as a result. They will not only surprise you, but encourage you. You will KNOW, not believe, but KNOW, that open, honest communication about very intimate subjects can, and will, change your life positively, and constructively.

ANI AND ELLIOT

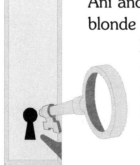

Ani and Elliot were an adorable, all-American, blonde and blue-eyed, smiling couple. They looked seventeen years old, although they were both 23 and had an 18-month-old baby. They had also both loved each other since the sixth grade. Although they were sure they would live "happily ever after," from time to time, they felt a strain between them. Because they did not want anything to ever happen to their love, they came to me, asking how they could make sure they would stay in love forever. In addition to other discussions we had, I asked them both to complete a questionnaire.

ANI'S RESPONSES:

1. *I wish I could show you that I love you more. Please tell me what I can do so that I can show you more love.*

2. *I wish you would pay more attention to me during our everyday lives. When I am cooking, come in and talk to me, and when I am with the baby at night, sit with us. I need more attention.*

3. *To me oral sex is something I really love; I like to do it to you and I love you to do it to me. I really would like more of it, too.*

4. *To me, anal sex is dirty. I am not interested and I'm glad you are not interested either. If you are, though, let me know. I do not want to close any doors unless we talk about it.*

5. *I would never take part in a threesome. I do not want to share you with anyone. But, if you are OK with it, I would not mind trying a vibrator during our lovemaking. What do you think?*

6. *I do have a fantasy, and it is kind of easy to accomplish. I want to play out the movie, "From Here to Eternity." I want to go to an isolated beach, kiss in the ocean, lie on the sand, and do everything they did. Then, I want you to carry me across the beach to our private cabin and take me body and soul. I actually dream about this. Do you think we can go away and do it?*

7. *What I really love is when you kiss me while we are having intercourse. I like to look in your eyes, feel your body, and your mouth. It makes everything more close and loving when we kiss.*

8. *After we make love, please tell me how you feel, tell me it was wonderful, or whatever else is on your mind. Hold me in your arms and talk about it; it's like having the pleasure again if you talk about it.*

9. *I will NEVER share you with another woman, or forgive you if you cheat on me. I can not ever forgive that.*

10. *I do not like when you rub my nipples, too, hard, especially when you kind of pinch them. I like you to just kind of stroke my nipples, not pull on them at all, please.*

Remember, when you read Elliot's responses, that Ani's responses are not in connection with his. His responses are totally independent of hers. After they completed their questionnaires they discussed the responses.

ELLIOT'S RESPONSES:

1. *I wish I could take more control during sex. I would like to tie you so that I feel in total control.*

2. *I wish you would ask me to take over, do whatever I want to you.*

3. *To me oral sex is fabulous. I love it, doing it to you, and you to me. I think this is a perfect part of our sex lives.*

4. *To me anal sex is a "don't touch, don't think" area. I find it kind of repulsive, and I would never have the nerve to, or even want to ask you for such a thing.*

5. *Threesomes are always interesting to any man, if it is with two women. Because I don't want anyone else, it is just a fantasy. But if you like the vibrator, then we can use that. I like it on my body as well. If you want to, we can both enjoy it.*

6. *My fantasy is that I wake up and you are sitting on top of me, with me hard as a rock and deep inside you. You are moving up and down on me as I hold your tits in my hands and watch as you have a really long orgasm.*

7. *What I really love is to watch you with the baby. I get so turned on sexually; some deep core inside of me gets hot and I feel like a million bucks. I feel so lucky and happy.*

8. *After we make love, please just hug me and let me go to sleep. I want to revel in the good feelings and let them take me to sleep, instead of disturbing them, I want to keep them.*

9. *I will NEVER hurt you, or insult you or deprive you in any way.*

10. *I don't like when you ask for more of something. If you want to go out more, make plans. If you want to kiss more, just kiss me more. If you want to have more friends, invite them, but don't put it on me, as though I'm responsible for giving you these things. You can take care of them for yourself.*

Ani and Elliot are an example of a couple without inhibitions or fears about sexuality. Their responses helped them to become even closer and to enjoy their lives even more fully.

Ani wanted to be able to show Elliot more love. She did it by saying yes to his request to take more control of their sex life. She even agreed to being tied once in a while, and to play act that she was his "love-slave." This increased passion in both of them.

Interestingly, Elliot loved watching Ani and the baby, and Ani wanted him to do more of that. They both responded well to these requests. Ani was overjoyed to know that Elliot felt intense joy when watching her and the baby. Elliot realized she wanted him to be more involved. Because he loved being involved, he did take part much more often, helping her in the kitchen, folding sheets together, etc.

Their responses confirmed they both loved oral sex and their distaste for anal sex. They did indeed begin to use a vibrator during their lovemaking, which intensified orgasms for Ani, and added stimulation for Elliot. He loved watching her pleasure herself before they made love. They both also loved the massages they gave each other.

Elliot made reservations in the Bahamas. They stayed in a two room bungalow on the beach, a short walk from the main hotel. They played *"From Here to Eternity"* three times during their five day stay.

Ani began to enjoy being awakened by the baby at night, because she could fulfill Elliot's fantasy. She would fellate Elliot until he became erect, then she would sit on him, moving to her own rhythm, looking at his ecstatic face. Both their fantasies were fulfilled. As Elliot said, "We'll share our fantasies from now on, and fulfill them as often as we can."

They compromised after making love. Although Ani wanted to talk and share, and Elliot wanted to quietly go to sleep, they agreed to alternate, so that each could be satisfied. Ani would curl up against Elliot's back, on their quiet evenings, and Elliot, leaning on his elbow, would look into Ani's eyes and tell her how wonderful everything was. Ani said, "It is so funny how just a word or two, and him looking deeply at me, is enough for me. I thought I needed an hour of talk and kissy-kissy stuff, but I don't. I just want that one moment of connection. Elliot understands and is really wonderful."

Both agreed that there would be no other person in their lives, and were grateful they both expressed this same belief. Ani also realized that she was in many ways looking to Elliot to make their lives together. His response to question ten, that she stop asking for more, but take it — turned on a light bulb in her head.

"As I read Elliots' responses," Ani related, "I felt as though I was growing up. I sat up straight and looked at him and told him 'you're on baby. From now on, I'm going to take what I want and not wait for you to get it or give it to me.'"

Not everyone was as exuberant about their responses, nor was everyone as responsive to each other's requests.

EVA AND TOM

A middle aged couple sat before me asking if they should see me or their lawyer. Eva was almost dowdy looking, dressed simply without any style. Her hair hung around her face as though she'd paid no attention to it at all. Although her sad eyes were huge, and her features rather pretty, her demeanor seemed to keep her faded in the background.

Tom, tall and lean, seemed to be very concerned about his looks. He sat very erect, and kept patting his perfectly groomed hair, playing with a huge gold bracelet on his right arm. They had been married 11 years without any real sense of joy or excitement.

"Tom and I are not compatible," Eva told me. "I don't think sex therapy is the answer for us. I don't really enjoy sex, I think it is very unimportant in a relationship, but Tom thinks it is the most important part. I was a 26-year-old virgin when we married, and Tom thought that was the most beautiful thing — that I had saved myself for him. Well, it was not like that at all, I just didn't have any interest. I love Tom and want to stay married to him, but sex is not my cup of tea."

"Eva is exaggerating a bit," Tom retorted. "She likes sex — the ordinary kind. I know she does. It is when I want to touch her or kiss her in certain places that she gets very upset. If we just had intercourse, I think she would be very happy."

I turned to Eva and she replied, "Oh, I guess he is right. I do like intercourse, but he wants me to kiss his member, and I will not do that. Believe it or not, he wants to kiss my vagina. Imagine that? I can not let him do such a thing."

Tom explained that Eva stopped paying attention to her appearance only four or five years ago. She is a very beautiful woman but she just doesn't seem to care anymore. After a few meetings Eva told Tom, "I thought it would be easier for you to stop wanting to do those things, if I did not look so good. I tried to make it easy for you."

Tom was astounded. I was, too. Often we do things at an unconscious level to mitigate certain circumstances. One of the most common is to remain overweight so that we avoid being seen as sexual objects. But, deliberately and consciously beginning a process of de-beautification is quite unusual. It is essential to remember, however, that Eva truly loved Tom very much.

I asked Eva to tell Tom why she began to look less attractive, other than to keep him from being interested sexually. She was quite flustered, saying she didn't understand my question. After a while she looked at me and then at Tom and said, "Because I felt he was suffering by being deprived of these things."

After a few minutes of silence I asked, "Why did you want to relieve what you conceived as his suffering?" The answer I expected and hoped for came forth.

"I love Tom," Eva explained. "I do not want to see him unhappy. I thought this would work for him."

It was then that the therapy could begin. We had established that there was love. And, where there is love, there is hope. We proceeded to use the desensitization techniques so that Eva would want Tom to kiss her entire body, and so that she could reciprocate.

Eva came a long way, actually enjoying kissing Tom's penis, and licking the tip, and around the rim. She did not want to take his penis into her mouth. He seemed perfectly satisfied with what she did enjoy doing. She also became very excited when he kissed her breasts and inner thighs, even enjoying his licking her toes. However, she truly felt uncomfortable if he attempted to kiss her vagina, other than the outside lips and her clitoris. Because Eva was multiple orgasmic each time Tom's tongue and lips merely touched her clitoris, she did not want him, as she said, "inside of me with his mouth."

The following are the answers to the questionnaires they completed after four weeks of therapy.

Eva's responses:

1. *I wish I could be more wild and free, and that you could accept me as I am until then.*

2. *I wish that you would love me as I am and love that I am changing as much as I can for you, and as much as I can for myself.*

3. *Oral sex is more acceptable, and you know that I love some of it, but please let's leave it as it is.*

4. *Anal sex is totally out of the question. I think if you had ever asked me for that I would have been out the door.*

5. *No threesomes — never — do not even think about it. I would like to try a vibrator for massages and for sex, too. Let's try. If you want to that is.*

6. *My fantasy is that we look at each other and are completely satisfied with what we see — no more changes, no more unhappiness.*

7. *What I really love is that you love me in spite of all our troubles.*

8. *After we make love, please do not make a big deal of it. Let's just enjoy it without talking it to death.*

9. *I will NEVER forget that I love you, and want our lives to be happy. That way I will keep learning and working with you, not against you, or against us.*

10. *I do not like you to try to do things that are out of bounds. We agree on things and I like to keep to our agreements; do not push me too far.*

TOM'S RESPONSES:

1. *I wish I could make you realize how much I want every part of you, in every way, because I love you.*

2. *I wish you would continue to loosen up and enjoy our bodies and our love.*

3. *To me oral sex is natural and beautiful. I love how much you do and how much you let me do now for you. Maybe someday we can do even more — but what we have now is wonderful. Thank you.*

4. *To me anal sex is something I do not really think about. I kind of put it in the category of homosexual sex. It is not for me, not really. Besides, I guess it is not for you at all, so that is fine with me.*

5. *I do not want another woman and certainly not another man. I would like to be massaged with a vibrator to relax me and to stimulate me, too. If you want to try it, I bet you would like it too. I hear women have great orgasms with vibrators.*

6. *My fantasy is to have you look the same way the day we were married. You were so gorgeous, so ravishing. There was a light inside of you, and I want to feel that love again. I want you as you were and as you are, too.*

7. *What I really love is that we are in love again. I was so scared that it was over between us. I love that you changed to help me, not because you did not care about me. I love more that you are looking beautiful again and changing again.*

8. *After we make love, please let's be grateful for what we have and for how life has changed for us. Let's not be ashamed to always be grateful and thankful, and be able to say so.*

9. *I will NEVER try to make you into someone different. It is you I love, and it is you, as you are, whom I will continue to love. I love that we are learning to appreciate each other and to meet each other's needs and I will NEVER let go of that knowledge.*

10. *I do not like you to be passive with me. I want you to always tell me what you want and how you want it. I do not want to feel that you are "giving in to me." I love that you want to change for me, and that you have, but I never want to feel that you are passive about any of the changes. I want to feel you are in control, for me and for yourself.*

Eva and Tom were very much in accord. They both wanted to satisfy each other, and accept each other as they were. They both appreciated their efforts in these directions.

Eva wanted to be able to be more of what Tom wanted in a sex partner, and Tom wanted her to know that he loved her as they were. Although he said he wanted her to be looser and freer, he was also satisfied to grant her, her wish that he be satisfied as things were. They both were willing and wanting to try using a vibrator during their lovemaking. Their fantasies were easily satisfied. Eva returned to her old vibrant, beautiful self. She actually loved looking stylish and beautiful. Although her "sacrifice" had been for Tom, she was thrilled to be able to let go of the "dowdy sexless look."

Tom told Eva in response to her fantasy, "I look at you with total pleasure and complete satisfaction. It is true that tomorrow will bring new joys to us because we are becoming closer and more loving. That does not mean that I am looking towards tomorrow, I am absolutely and completely thankful for today."

When Eva understood why Tom wanted to express his feelings after making love, it was more acceptable to her. She had thought he wanted to get turned on again, rather than realizing he wanted to appreciate what they had just experienced.

Both Eva and Tom had difficulty with their responses to question number ten. Eva had expressed herself clearly, she wanted to set limits, and not be pushed. Tom said he wanted her to be less passive, even though Eva said, "I am not passive. I am telling you exactly what I want and do not want." Tom said after a while that he needed to be reassured, to be told that Eva was changing for herself as well as for him.

He did not want to feel that it was all for him. When Eva said she loved the changes, but was in control of which changes she would make, Tom was relieved. He wanted to feel they were both benefiting from the therapy, not that it was a sacrifice on Eva's part.

Eva's attitudes about what is right and wrong about sex came from her childhood. She was punished because she was touching herself in the bathtub when she was six years old. She was dressed very plainly during her school years and her mother often said, "Remember Eva, you do not want to look like you want something that you do not want."

Eva laughingly told us she was not quite sure what her mother meant by that; it surprised her that the statement had such a profound effect on her.

When she wanted to relieve Tom of the sexual urges she felt she couldn't satisfy, she began to dress so that she would not "look like she wanted something she did not want."

Eva and Tom had lost the most important aspect of their marriage and lives. They had lost the memory and knowledge of their love. As soon as their love was evidenced, they took control of their lives and created the improvements needed to cement and continue the love.

Too often, we lose track and stray. Take back what you had on your wedding day. Reignite the passion, respect and remember what you felt as you took your vows. Using this renewal energy, talk to each other and find a way back to the complete joy you felt, and can feel again. Work at it. Strive for it. Do not take it for granted, or give it up without great effort.

It is your life, do not be frivolous with it. Do not waste it, and certainly don't trash it. It is not a dress rehearsal you know — your life is a one shot deal. So, do what you do with love and affection and respect, and with determination and effort. Do it for yourself and do it for each other. Feel the love, and keep the love. Use every tool and technique you can! Don't lose it as Eva and Tom almost did. Look back to the joyful days, and then look forward to all the possibilities you have with each other.

ELLIE AND JASON

 Jason's father and mother were very cruel to each other and to their children. Jason's brother left home when he was 14. His sister left when she was not quite 15, and Jason left a few days after his sister, when he was just 12 years old, to join her, and travel around the country, working at menial jobs. They found their brother a year later in Atlanta, Georgia, living with an aunt they had only heard about, but had never met.

The three of them sat for hours telling of the torture in their home. They talked about a drunken father beating on them and their mother, and wild sex scenes, which would start with passion and apparent pleasure, but end with their mother screaming in pain from a beating, which came after the orgasm.

Why did their mother put up with it they wondered again and again. They never found out; their mother died of a heart attack, just two years after Jason left. They had no interest in ever seeing their father again, nor, apparently, did he care about them.

Ellie, on the other hand, had a lovely white picket fence childhood. Her father was an engineer, her mother was a homebody, and she and her siblings were perfect, story book children. She remembers baking in the kitchen every day, dinners as a family unit, and lots of laughter, communication, and love.

Then she met Jason, he fell madly and passionately in love with her, and she with him. She had never known anyone like him. He was volatile, exciting, handsome, and successful; he had it all. She couldn't want for more. When she told her parents, they warned her about his temper and his brooding moods; he walked out during a family dinner once because the rice was too hard for his taste. "I don't have to put up with this abuse," he announced and walked out. Everyone was shocked. How could hard rice be seen as abusive? But, because Ellie was in love, she did not take these incidents seriously. They married six months after they met. She was 22 and he, 27. They made a beautiful couple; she had red hair and fair skin and he was dark with olive skin. Her blue eyes were almost the exact color of his. They liked to tell people that their children were meant to be, to continue the perfect color of blue.

Because old habits and childhood memories die hard, Jason loved Ellie so much that it hurt him. Sadly, it hurt him the same way his love for his mother hurt him. When he tried to show her love, he got a slap or a push away. When he wanted her to show him love, she would laugh at him. He remembered when he was eight years old, he asked her to kiss him because he had earned straight "A's" on his report card. She smacked him across the face instead and said, "You will remember a smack more than you will remember a kiss, and you will keep getting "A's" because you will remember it so well."

Jason's attitude about love had been twisted and perverted into a mass of ugly and distorted beliefs. These attitudes affected his behavior, which was atrocious. Ellie was ready to leave him, abandoning all of her dreams and hopes, accepting that Jason was never going to be the "man of her dreams." She asked for my help, to lessen the pain of leaving him. She loved him very much in spite of his behavior, but she was smart enough to know that she could not stay with him unless he changed.

We worked towards that change. Ellie was very receptive to therapy since she was so in love, desperately seeking a common path on which they could travel towards happiness together. Jason, on the other hand, had created a defensive structure, which was almost impenetrable. When he entered my office, I was struck with his rugged good looks, from his black hair to his silver tip boots. His chest stuck out, and his head was held high. His entire demeanor announced, "Don't even try to get near me, I won't let you."

I knew Jason needed one of my "axes" right between his eyes. I waited for a few minutes while he arrogantly said Ellie wasn't going to tell him what to do, and that he was ready to walk out right then and there.

"You're starting with the wrong guy if you think you are going to push me around," he said directly to Ellie. She began to cry, and looked towards me for help.

"You feel great seeing Ellie cry don't you? It's familiar territory. Women cry, and men abuse them. Isn't that the way life is?" I asked, surprising both of them with my "ax." Although I knew nothing of Jason's past when I said this, his behavior and demeanor made me believe he grew up watching his father abuse his mother. Without that background, he would not be acting the way he was; I was sure of it. That is why I threw the "ax" as directly as I could. I also knew there was a small glimmer of hope for this couple. If Jason did not love Ellie, he would not have come for therapy at all. I prayed their love would bring them through, and my "ax" would light the way.

Jason looked at me, his eyes wide. "Do you believe that?" he asked in a very surprised voice.

"I know that you believe that," I answered, letting him take it in, as Ellie sat silently, not knowing what to say, or what was happening.

Jason stood up, hitching his belt with his two thumbs like John Wayne, and said, "Well you are full of shit. That is not how life is supposed to be. We are supposed to love each other. I ran away when I was a kid to get away from abuse; I certainly do not believe that is how I am supposed to live, and I do not want to live that way."

"Then why are you such an abusive bastard," I asked, deliberately following his lead by using abusive language.

"I am not any such thing," he shouted. As Ellie began to cry again, he screamed at her, "What the hell are you crying about?"

"You are abusive," I retorted. You are screaming at her. Let's see if you can go over to Ellie, take her in your arms, and gently ask her why she is crying, instead of screaming at her like a vicious creep?"

Again, I was pushing the edge, calling him names and challenging him to see what and who he was.

"No one is going to push me around — no one," he began to shout in a firm, strong voice. But, when he repeated the words "no one," his voice cracked and he began to cry. As he sobbed uncontrollably for a full three minutes, I held Ellie, not allowing her to go to him. If I allowed her to play nursemaid, she would have broken the intense feelings, and lost the moment forever; he needed to go through this alone in order to have a breakthrough. I held on to her, both of us watching as Jason sobbed like a baby.

The therapy began. Jason told the entire story, the abuse, the pain, the abandonment, all of it. He told of the hardships he endured until he found his aunt and of the grief he felt losing his mother before he ever felt any love from her. He also told of his fear and his determination to be strong and in control, so that he could never again be hurt.

Jason reminisced about how all of his fantasies came true when he met Ellie, the woman of his dreams, who had the family of his dreams. But, because his fears controlled him, he pushed away the best things that had ever happened to him. His behavior, which was being controlled by his unconscious, was cruel and vicious to those around him and of course, to himself.

His love for Ellie, his intelligence and his determination to make life work for him were the foundation of his change. Jason turned back the evil demons of his childhood and forced his adult self to take over. Their therapy succeeded, and Jason's life was forever changed through love. After five weeks of therapy, they completed the questionnaire.

ELLIE'S RESPONSES:

1. *I wish I could take away all of your bad memories. Because I can not, I promise that from now on, everything will be perfect for us.*

2. *I wish you would remember to live in the moment, live for the now, and please give me more massages.*

3. *To me oral sex is really wonderful, especially when you do it. I am only half kidding - I like to do it to you, too.*

4. *To me anal sex is strange, and out of my loop, but you know what, let's try it if you want to, we will ask Carole about it.*

5. *NO! NO! NO! I never want a threesome; I want you all to myself, although the vibrator is something we can both share. Do you want to?*

6. *My fantasy is that you buy me a long fur stole. I ring the doorbell, and, when you open the door, you are stark naked and I am wearing only my fur stole. We start to dance and I kind of perform for you as the "leopard lady." (If the stole is leopard, or the mink lady, or whatever.) Anyhow, I dance and tease you,*

and touch you with the soft fur, and we both get crazy and finally make love on the stole. As soon as you buy me one of these, we will do it. OK?

7. What I really love, is knowing how much you love me. I hope you will always show that love every day and I promise you I will show you the love I feel for you all the time.

8. After we make love, please get a really hot washcloth and wash my vagina and legs. I love that feeling. And if you are not too tired, a little hot oil on my belly would be nice, too.

9. I will NEVER stop loving you and I will NEVER say no to you, as long as you love me as you do today. I can not think of anything I do not want to do with you (except threesomes).

10. I do not like when you ignore me when I am talking about stupid things. I like to tell you gossip and everyday stuff, and I would like you to listen. I know you tune me out when I talk about things that do not interest you. Oh yes, I do not like when you rub one spot for too long. I like you to move your fingers around — that goes for your lips and tongue, too. I hope you do not mind my telling you these things. I love you.

JASON'S RESPONSES:

1. *I wish I could make love to you more often. Is it alright if we make love every day, or is that too much?*

2. *I wish you would be more aggressive during our lovemaking; I would like you to ask for what you want and do more to me.*

3. *To me oral sex is an absolute must. I love it.*

4. *To me anal sex is dirty. I do not even think about it.*

5. *I do not ever want anyone in bed with us. It is you and me always, no one else. What about a vibrator? Do you want to use one?*

6. *My fantasy is that we make believe we are little kids and we make love as though we do not know what we are doing. You explore me and I explore you, and we play at finding out how and what to do.*

7. *What I really love is lying around in bed with you in the morning and at night. I feel so safe with you.*

8. *After we make love, please tell me you loved it and that it was the best sex you ever had. I love to hear you talk about how good it was and how much you loved it.*

9. *I will NEVER cheat on you, and I will NEVER hurt you or ask you to do anything you do not want to do. I know that I do not ever want to play at bondage or S&M. It scares me.*

10. *The only thing you do that I do not like happens during oral sex. I would love you to touch me all over while you are kissing my penis, instead of just sucking. Touch my balls and nipples, and rub my body with your hands. I love when you rub my penis while you are sucking me. I love when you touch me, and I do not like it when you don't.*

Jason and Ellie laughed a great deal as they read their responses. They both loved how adamant they were about never cheating on each other or even considering a threesome. Jason was a bit uncomfortable about trying a vibrator, but as Ellie told me later, "He's so wonderful, he is willing to try anything. And you know what, he liked it."

Ellie was shocked that she was not touching Jason as she fellated him. "I guess I was so engrossed, I did not realize my hands were just lying there most of the time," she told me. "I love to touch Jason, and I will now that I am aware of it."

Jason asked where he could get a hot washcloth, and we all laughed at that. Ellie agreed to keep a washcloth in the bathroom sink in very hot water, so that it would be ready for Jason. He in turn agreed to be sure it was still hot. Performing this ritual has become one of the most loving and caring times for them. As Jason cleanses Ellie, he watches her satisfied face, her lovely body, and he feels a wonderful sense of giving something that is very much appreciated. Ellie has also arranged a hot oil cup, which she keeps on the night table. It is a commercial dish, which has a candle under the oil container. They both rub a bit of oil on each other before they go to sleep.

Remember that this does not have to be done with great vigor and energy. A bit of oil on your fingers, a touch here and there, is more than enough; it says so much.

Ellie is not at all interested in S&M or bondage and has relieved Jason by telling him so. They both understand why such behavior would frighten him. If you have a background of anger and abuse, it is not a good idea to replay it in any way. Old memories and behaviors can take over, causing you to lose control. As you have read, it can happen when you least expect it. Remember Lillian and Debbie?

Ellie admitted she felt silly telling Jason how great a lover he was, and how much he satisfied her. She liked that he wanted to hear it since it gave her permission to, as she said, "I love getting all gushy and mushy after sex now that I know you like it," she told Jason, "I will say it more often."

Their fantasies are truly in tune with each other and have been played out with great gusto and pleasure. Jason bought Ellie a "leopard" stole which is seven feet long and four feet wide. He had it made of "leopard velvet." She has become a very sultry, dancing seductress, and enjoys it so much, she teases Jason that she is going to become a topless dancer.

His fantasy is fun for both of them, since they feel so cared for by each other. As they play baby to each other, they take great care in washing each other, licking and kissing, dressing and undressing, asking questions and giving answers — all of which adds up to new experiences and new awareness.

One of their favorite "baby" experiences involves asking, "Does little baby like this?" It is very easy for the answer to be "Yes," or "No, little baby does not like this." As I explained in the case of Julia, we take on a persona with which we're comfortable in doing the things or saying the things we really find uncomfortable. This is what enabled Ellie and Jason to fulfill his fantasy of playing "baby." It allows them to be very honest with each other, asking for things they might not be comfortable with in their own persona. It also allows the "pretend" baby Jason to have the love and attention he never received as the "real" baby Jason.

Ellie told me that she was able to ask Jason, in her itty bitty baby voice, "Oh honey, baby needs ou to suckie suck, harder on that spot. Baby likey ou to really suckie hard now." She blushed as she told me, saying that she could never have said that in her real adult voice.

Ellie and Jason are happy, sexually in tune with each other and very grateful that they did not just give up. Their situation truly seemed impossible; Ellie was a gentle, soft woman who would not allow herself to be mistreated in any way. Her upbringing demanded that she be treated in accordance with her self-image and ego. Even though Jason's behavior was totally unacceptable, she wanted to make every effort before she gave him up. Her efforts paid off since Jason loved her enough to work his way out of his horrific childhood and into self-possessed manhood with a mind of his own. The angry, destructive child was looked at, unaccepted and dismissed, as the man finally took over successfully and completely.

It is truly difficult to communicate with another human being on a deeply intimate level. It is threatening and frightening. I like to use the analogy of a person who holds out his hand to another. He is taking a great risk that the other person will not accept his hand, and that he will be left looking foolish, his hand hanging in mid-air, obvious to the entire world, rejected and ignored. On the other hand, if he does not extend his hand, although he will not have to face rejection, he will not be able to revel in acceptance.

We must extend ourselves, take the risk, and make the attempt if we want to be held by a warm and loving person. Love does not fly into your room through the window; you must be out there giving off energy and signals of warmth and acceptance. Take a chance and put yourself on a shelf for observation and perusal.

After you do find a lover, however, the work truly begins. Talk to each other of your dreams and desires. Talk to each other of your needs and wants. Do not be afraid to take these risks early in the relationship. Your partner cannot know what you think or feel. You must tell him or her. If you do not talk early, you will suffer later. So many couples marry without truly sharing their deepest, most intimate needs. These couples are doomed to failure, if not a very superficial, unrewarding life together.

REMEMBER:

Do not try to play beautiful music on the piano unless you use the black as well as the white keys. Show *every* facet of your personality, share secrets and express *every* feeling, if you want a complete and loving life together. Take risks and be truly intimate; the payoff is worth it.

CHAPTER FIVE

The ♂♀ Conclusion

THE ORGASM: The physiological response of the body to a variety of physical stimulations; the transcendence of all; the sharing of loving feelings in a giving and taking of energy and excitement; a circular flow which has no equal; a moment in space and time during which we are completely released — no tensions, worries, or fears; the phenomenon most misunderstood and most discussed.

We all want it. We all need it. We all seek it. I feel very strongly that we must all recognize that it is not the orgasm which is the goal of a relentless search, it is what the orgasm means to us. During an orgasm we are completely relaxed, out of control and in a state of Nirvana. We need this feeling in order to perpetuate our feelings of safety. During an orgasm, we are close and intimate, and warm and self-confident; we are one with another person, a person with whom we bond with in very deep emotional ways. We need this bond; we seek what the orgasm represents and the feelings it reaffirms for us. We seek the joy of the intimacy, and the profundity of that which we have shared. The orgasm, as fulfilling and wondrous as it is, is even so much more. It is an expression of ourselves as complete and satisfied loving human beings. It is a moment of bliss — an affirmation of our love of life, of ourselves, and of our lover.

Although billions of words have been written in an infinite number of books, the subject of sex is still riveting. We all want to know how to be more sexual human beings, and how to enjoy our sexuality more fully. Towards these ends, we read about it, we talk about it, and we attempt to learn about it.

From the Files of a Sex Therapist has brought you to the subject of sex through the eyes of ordinary men and women who, in extraordinary ways, have found complete fulfillment and satisfaction. They fought hard, they suffered hard, and they achieved their goal. Those who did not strive with every fiber of energy in their beings did not succeed and sadly did not achieve their goal.

It is an absolute truth that we are all different in an infinite number of ways. We are especially different in our sexual styles, our sexual choices and our sexual pleasures. Please do not expect something from yourself which you do not really want. Do not allow media pressure, television, movies, or even books like this one, to make demands on you with which you are uncomfortable. The point is, the only essential element in your sexuality and sexual pleasures is YOU. The problem is that too many of us do not really know what we want or how we want it. Or, if we do, we do not know how to get it. Do you?

I try, throughout these pages to give you information about human sexuality through the eyes of the men and women who have sought my help. I try to offer you ideas, alternatives, choices, and mainly a perspective on sexuality so that you can see it clearly and intelligently, through YOUR own eyes, not through mine, or anyone else's. All that I ask in this chapter, is that you read each word, and answer each question, with your heart.

There are parameters which you can follow as you try to follow your heart and your physical needs towards greater intimacy and sexual pleasures. There is pleasure for everyone, in every way that they choose to have it. If, as I have said many times, you do not hurt yourself or anyone else, then you are doing what is right for YOU. IF, however, you are not being honest with yourself, and you are depriving or even punishing yourself in some way, only YOU know that. Dig deep. Look through your own eyes, not the eyes of your childhood. Make your own choices, not the choices of any outside pressures. Be true to YOU, as you go through life asking and answering questions. You are the only one with the right answers.

You have read about the people just described. You know what they have been through and what they have gained because of their efforts. The question at this point is, what do you want? What are you willing to do to get there? Please answer the following questions before going on to the next page. The responses will help you to focus on your sexual and sensual attitudes, so that you can look for specific answers, to specific needs.

WHAT ARE YOUR SEXUAL PLEASURES?

1. Sexually I am_____(satisfied, dissatisfied, etc.)
2. What I need sexually is_____.
3. If I could_____I would be more sexually satisfied.
4. My inhibitions are_____.
5. I am sexually anoretic (not interested) when_____.
6. My sexual feelings depend on_____.
7. I feel sexual sadness when_____.
8. Emotions and sex are_____.
9. My favorite sexual act is_____.
10. I need my partner to_____.

Two of my clients responded to these questions as follows:

GEORGE

1. *Sexually I am very ordinary I think. I do not care much about it. It is OK. My wife and I have sex every week or so, but it is no great thing. We feel closer when we do, and I feel relaxed, but it is tiring, and really no big deal.*

2. *Sexually I need some kissing and hugging, and a climax either by intercourse or oral sex. I like Hollie to climax and enjoy it, too. That makes it better for me.*

3. *If I could, I would take a pill to turn myself on more often. I do not think it would change much. There is nothing I really want that I am not getting now.*

4. *My inhibitions are not in my consciousness. I think I am pretty free. I walk around nude, have oral sex, and lots of touching, etc. I do not like anal sex, but who does? I do not like other men — is that an inhibition? I guess I am not wild and a sex machine. Is that an inhibition?*

5. *I am not interested in sex most of the time. I'm 41, and it is no big deal. When we are close, we have sex and it is great. We do not seem to miss it, or want more. Once a week or every ten days seems enough for Hollie and I.*

6. *My sexual feelings depend on my energy level, how Hollie is acting, if the kids are out of the house, if things went well at work, all of it.*

7. *I feel sexual sadness — I do not know. I guess I remember when it was more passionate with Hollie and I. I would like that back again. How can I get that back?*

8. *Emotions and sex are separate I guess, but now that I think about it, sex is very tied up with how I am feeling towards Hollie and towards myself.*

9. *My favorite sexual act is feeling attached, like one person, when I am inside Hollie and we just hold on to each other very closely. As I write about this I realize how*

much I love the sex act. Why I don't do it more is a good question for me to ask.

10. *I need Hollie to take control. If she wants it more often, we will do it more often.*

George's responses are very interesting. Notice that as he thinks about his sexual life, he becomes more interested. He realizes what he truly enjoys. He realizes how emotions control him, but he also recognizes that Hollie could control him if she chose to. On the surface George is a sexual person, with limited sexual drive. However, he would like to increase this sexual drive through his wife. If she takes control, he can become interested more frequently.

Working with George and Hollie was easy. As soon as each of them recognized that their sex life was satisfying, but infrequent, and more importantly that George was interested in more frequent sex, things began to change. Hollie accepted the gauntlet George had thrown and became more aggressive sexually. She set the scene a few times a week, and George responded.

The underlying truth here is that George thought he had no inhibitions, but indeed he had. Initiating sex was difficult for him. As soon as Hollie was given permission to be the aggressor, her inhibitions were ameliorated as were George's. Answering these questions, is, on the surface, a simple task. But look deeply into the responses, and find your real truth, your real needs.

Sally

1. *Sexually I am just not interested. I can not believe Tony is even here asking you to help us. There is no big deal in this.*

2. *What I need sexually is to be left alone.*

3. *If I could, I would get a massage every night and be very satisfied.*

4. *I do not have any inhibitions. I just do not think there is any big deal about sexual intercourse.*

5. *I am not interested in sex at any time really. Like I said — no big deal.*

6. *My sexual feelings depend on if I feel loved and secure. I never thought of that but sometimes I do feel like having sex when I am really happy.*

7. *I feel sexual sadness when we have had intercourse and it is over. There is no more contact, no intimacy as they say.*

8. *Emotions and sex are all wrapped up together.*

9. *My favorite sexual act is oral sex, but Tony does not like to do that.*

10. *I need Tony to love me more often out of the bedroom. In fact, I want him to show he loves me all of the time. Showing me love when he wants sex is not enough for me.*

Sally's responses are very typical. Because Tony and she do not share the warmth and intimacy of a loving sexual experience, Sally has convinced herself she is not a sexual person. However, she is orgasmic, she participates actively, and she enjoys the sex she does experience. She says, "it is no big deal" because there is a sadness connected with her enjoyment. She wants more.

When she and Tony shared their responses, they also shared a very deep connection, which they had not been aware of for years. Sally's facade of being asexual was dropped almost immediately. Tony's facade of being, as he said, "an in and out man" was also dropped. Tony had always been afraid of "not being a really good soul partner." He felt if he made the least amount of sexual effort, he would never disclose any sexual inadequacies. Tony said, "I always thought that if I tried something, or was too lovey dovey, I would be a big jerk and I would be embarrassed."

Both Sally and Tony suffered from inhibitions in different ways. When they were able to share their thoughts, they felt safer with each other, and were able to satisfy each other more frequently and more completely.

The word communication has been done and redone. I, myself, am tired of hearing it as the solution to problems. But you know what, it is the solution to most problems. Bringing a problem to the light of day is the only way to solve it. The only way to bring it to the light of day is to tell each other what it is. If you walk into a dark room, the first thing you do is flip the switch. Well, flip the switch. Answer these questions, share the responses, and fill each others needs.

This does not in any way imply that you should be doing or feeling anything. There are no "shoulds" or judgements. All that is implied here is that you make an effort to discover what you are truly comfortable with and what you truly need. Uncover your own "sexual ghosts;" look at your inhibitions or your fears. Discover what you and your partner can do and what you are willing to do to reach sexual satisfaction.

Throughout the years, couples have shared their most intimate secrets with me. What is the truth about the sex lives of the men and women who live their lives as you and I do? Let's really look at them. Let's be honest.

Is sex the big bang, the lightening and the bells? Does the earth move and do the stars rotate at breakneck speed? Of course they do, but very rarely. Can there be good sex without love? Of course there can. Remember that one night stand when all the glory of the world was focused in your body or the one or two nights when you felt angry, or sad, or hateful, but the sex was absolutely wondrous?

Remember the hundreds of nights during which you lay next to your partner, fuming about something he or she said or did. Think about how you could have changed from feeling distant and alienated to feeling warm and close. What could you have done? What are you willing to do the next time your emotions stand in the way of your sexual and sensual needs?

What power do we have when our anger stands in the way of our sexual pleasure? What choices do we have if we are sad, or tired, or upset? How do we find our own piece of sexual heaven despite all of the normal impediments, which seem to stand in the way?

It is true, that if we can let go of the emotions which constrain us from personal pleasure, we can also be emotionally healthier. Holding on to anger or fear or sadness, is emotionally as well as sexually crippling. Sex without love, with anger, with fear, is certainly possible. But, it is not too probable. Most of us are emotional beings, our feelings are superimposed on ALL of our behaviors. Who we were as children, how we behaved, and what we were taught, keeps control of us too strongly and too frequently. If we can let go and realize what is holding us back, we can truly be freer and more satisfied.

If we keep in mind that we deserve the physical pleasure of sexual contact, we may be able to let go of the emotions which keep us from that pleasure. If we remember that our emotions are within our choice, we can then choose to feel warm and loving so that we will desire and enjoy sexual contact. In case you do not believe that emotions are a choice, think about the time you felt really hurt and sad and lonely. Suddenly the phone rang, and a friend invited you to dinner. You quickly changed your attitude. What happened to the hurt and sad and lonely? It was replaced by the feeling of being wanted and included. These feelings are positive. These feelings were chosen above the more negative and destructive ones.

Think about the time you were enraged at your boss. You wanted to kill him or her. You had thoughts of putting their head through a wall, while you screamed and threatened and ranted and raved. What did you choose to do? You chose to express a reposed, confident look, with a smile on your face and a gracious handshake. Or, at the very most you were able to say quietly, "I am upset, but I will deal with it." You chose the feeling you needed to express, and if you remember, the anger subsided as you pretended to feel calm.

There are a multitude of experiments which prove that we not only can choose a feeling, but the feeling we pretend to have, becomes so real to us it actually influences our physiology. If we make believe that we are going to meet someone we love, we fantasize about the meeting and think about what we will do when we are together. Although it is all make believe, our physiology responds positively. Our immune system improves, our blood pressure drops, our stomach acidity drops, our feelings actually change so that we are feeling happier and more excited.

If, on the other hand you pretend to be angry or upset, the exact opposite will happen. Your white blood cells will decrease, your blood pressure will rise, and your stomach acidity will increase. Remember when you were a kid and didn't want to go to school. You would make believe you were sick. Remember how sick you really felt when you were telling your mom how bad your head hurt, or how your stomach was killing you. You actually convinced yourself you could not possibly go to school. Remember?

Well, this is true of all feelings. We choose to have them, and we choose to keep them. You have the choice. If sexual pleasure is out of the question for you when you are upset, you can pretend that you are not upset. You can use sexual and intimate gestures to help you to leave the negative mood and enter the passionate one. In other words, you are what you pretend to be. You pretend to be what you want to be.

Moment by moment you build your life. You build it as you want to live in it. Make each brick, each nail, each roof tile count for you. Do not waste any of the tools you have. All of them are YOUR life. Emotions allowed to take control of you, are emotions which cause illness, waste time, and drain your energy.

MAKE LIFE HAPPEN:

☑ Understand your own power and use it to create a better life for yourself. You can do it.

☑ Share your understanding and your power with your partner. You can both do it.

☑ Live each day with the goal of loving each other in every way.

☑ Remind each other of that goal. Behave as though you are conscious of that goal.

☑ Recognize what your partner does to indicate he or she is remembering the goal of loving each other.

In order to help you to understand these ideas, I want to share the following answers to this question: *How did you manage to continue your romantic love and keep your sex lives active and satisfying?*

Sidney

"After 41 years of marriage, we still have intercourse about once a week, and it is good. But you know sex is a more inclusive thing for us, not just intercourse. If I touch Jenny's behind as we walk up the stairs, or if she touches my nipples and laughs as she always does - these are sexual moments for us. We never go to sleep without talking about how we feel. If there was anger or fights or disappointments, we talk about it. I remember what you said about play-acting, and I often pretend I am Kirk Douglas. How could Kirk Douglas not be a sexy, romantic guy, even if he is a little angry or upset?"

Jenny

"Sid and I care about each other. We like each other. So when I hate him or we have a big fight, I remember how I really feel, and I show him the positive side of me. Oh, we fight, I scream and get it all out. But then I help him to make up with me and we laugh about what happened. I guess we have been such good friends for so long, we understand each other very well. That is the essential element, understanding each other. Making love is so natural when you show you care, and that is what we do."

Henry

"Sex for me after 12 years together is really the icing on the cake. Sometimes I want it and it is delicious, but sometimes, I just want the cake, or sometimes I do not want anything at all. That is when I use the ideas I learned here. I act especially nice to Gloria. I pay attention to her, and that makes me remember how beautiful she is, and then I see her as very desirable. It is funny, but the less sexual I feel, the more romantic I become. Then I become sexy - one leads to the other."

Gloria

"It is really wonderful that we both know how to satisfy each other. We can argue and feel distant for a while like anyone else, but we know that we do not want to extend bad feelings. So Henry or I reach out. It does not seem to matter who takes the first step. We both welcome it. It is so much better to be happy with each other. I can not even imagine how we used to be, angry and distant for weeks at a time. It was horrible. And you know, it is not that sex is better or more frequent that is so good. It is that we show each other that we like each other. We always did like each other, but now we show it."

Harvey

"Marge is what sex means to me, so with Marge, my sex life is active. She is life and laughter and hugs and orgasms. She is romance and love. How could life not be good with Marge? She makes it so."

Marge

"We came a long way for Harvey to say what he just said. It was not always like that. Our first two years were hell. I left him three times, but my mother would not let me give up. She said that marriage was a commitment and I had to stick with it. I am glad I did, but it was hard work, believe me. We have been together nine years now and each day I think about what I will do to keep it this good. I really plan it. Not a day *goes by that I do not have one special surprise for Harvey, or he for me. Silly things, a note in his underwear, a phone call with some suggestive remarks, a flower from the garden next to his toast. I do easy things that do not cost any money, but I do them. It is worth it. We both feel respected and admired and worthy of attention. That is what is so wonderful. We are both worthy of attention."*

Rick

"Being married to Carole is not easy. She wants to understand everything I do and say. She wants to discuss behaviors and motives and looks and voice tone. Each day we sit on the patio and take about ten minutes to recap our relationship. We are usually light and happy as we re-affirm feelings and express our needs. Sometimes, it is heavy and terrible and hard for me because I am not like her. But always, it is fruitful. We get to the bottom of things, we do not let things slide. I think it is because we are so honest with each other about our feelings and our needs that we are as happy as we are. It is always an adventure and unusual, but it is also always wonderful in the end. I learn so much by expressing my feelings. It is amazing how life has changed since expressing my feelings. We keep our romance and our sex life as good as it is because we are honest with each other. Carole said to me once, "If you respect yourself and me, you will trust me enough to share with me, not hold back stuff which can erode our good feelings." I think she is absolutely right about that. I used to hold back a lot of stuff, and my relationships did not work the way this one is. When you respect each other you can trust each other with all of your feelings. Sharing it all makes it work."

Carole

"I am a therapist, and I do have a great deal of experience. When Rick and I were married, I tried to impart some of my philosophy. We made a contract to talk every day for a few minutes. We contracted to be honest, to share, and to make every attempt to explore our feelings - positive and negative as they came up. It has been working for us and I know that it works for everyone. When your feelings are out in the open, the bad ones go away and the good ones prevail. It is the good feelings that inspire desire and passion. I want desire and passion in life, so I keep the feelings as clear as possible."

What have we learned? Talk to each other frequently and intensely. Know what you are thinking and feeling and share it with your partner. Know what your needs are and become aware of them on a daily basis. Do not sweep yourself under a rug. Act as though you deserve whatever you want and need. Act so that you can get whatever you want and need.

You get what you give, since love and kindness are the lures for love and kindness. If you cast these feelings onto the waters of your life, that is what will come back to you. But if you do not love yourself, and feel kindly to yourself, how can you feel that way towards others.

☑ Look in the mirror and tell yourself that you are wonderful. After a while, you will realize that you are truly wonderful. We all are.

☑ Look in the mirror and ask, "What do I need? What do I want?" Do this everyday for a minute. You will get answers, believe me.

☑ Tell your partner that you are wonderful.

☑ Tell your partner what you want and need.

☑ Plan a program together to achieve your mutual goals.

Relationships are complicated, difficult and impossible, and easy, simple and wonderful. Your relationship will be all of these. It will move from the glorious to the excruciating. None of us are immune to the roller coaster of feelings and experiences. Life moves us in many directions all of the time, but we have control of the length of time we stay in the dale — until we climb the hill. Take life by the hand and lead it where you want it to go. If you are angry, and you will be — be angry. Let it out. Talk about it. Try to relieve the causes of the anger and LET IT GO!

If you are sad, be sad. Cry and keen, and weep and sob. Talk about it. Try to relieve the cause of the sadness, and LET IT GO!

The expression God grant me the wisdom to know the difference between what I can and cannot change is extremely brilliant. If it cannot be changed — LET IT GO!

From The Files of A Sex Therapist was written so that the lessons learned by others can be learned by YOU as well. This book was written so that I could share the joys of so many people. I hope that you will see the ways you can grab life and take what you want from it. I hope the tragedies will warn you and your loved ones and keep you safe from such agony. I hope the triumphs will be inspiration to you. YOU DESERVE IT ALL! I hope you find bliss which is different from happiness. Happiness depends on the circumstances, the environment, the context of your life. Bliss is a feeling you have within you all of the time. It cannot be taken away regardless of the circumstances.

When tragedies, problems or stress occur, reach inside for your bliss and hold it very tightly. Those moments will pass, the circumstances will change, and happiness will return. Bliss will help you along the way. I wish you bliss.

 # Epilogue

THANK YOU FOR READING my book *From the Files of A Sex Therapist*. I want to share with you that I am fully aware that the problems you may be having seem overwhelming and impossible to overcome. I want you to know that most people who go for help feel the same way. Trust me, you can overcome whatever it is that you are experiencing. Try to incorporate some of the ideas on these pages. Try to work towards the solutions with all the trust and love you can find within you. Try to be who you want to be, and create the life you want for yourself. Do not give up. Do not feel hopeless or helpless. There is no such thing. We all have power, we have to find it, not fear it, and then use it.

Seek help. Therapy is short term and very effective. Talk to your partner. Reach out to each other. And think about the 3 R's of great sex:

RESPECT — If you feel respect for each other and treat each other accordingly, you will both touch the stars. There is nothing as wonderful as respecting and being respected. It is indicative of maturity, love, responsibility, and intense kindness. Do It! Be respectful.

RECOGNITION — Everyone of us needs to be recognized. We need to know that you notice us. Tell your partner you realize how hard they work, you like the new furniture arrangement, you enjoyed dinner, you appreciate how tired he or she must be, you realize the efforts made to plan the picnic, etc. If we are ignored and not recognized, it is very rare that we feel warm and loving and sexual. But if we are noticed, we feel good about ourselves, and when we do, we feel sexual and loving.

REWARD — Give rewards graciously, frequently, and honestly. Compliments are food for our psyche. Our ego swells with pride when we are told something is good, wonderful, attractive or exciting. Be generous with rewards. Your generosity is a velvet runway to a more loving and caring partner. Reward because you want to. Reward because you notice that the reward is deserved. Reward because you are so full of love and abundance that you hold nothing in. When you give you will receive.

With love and warmth and hope for good loving,

carole altman